THE FALL AT HOME

The Fall at Home

NEW AND COLLECTED APHORISMS

Don Paterson

FABER & FABER

First published in 2018
by Faber & Faber Ltd
Bloomsbury House
74–77 Great Russell Street
London WC1B 3DA

Typeset by Typo•glyphix
Printed in England by CPI Group (UK) Ltd, Croydon, CR0 4YY

The right of Don Paterson to be identified as author of this work
has been asserted in accordance with Section 77 of the Copyright,
Designs and Patents Act 1988

A CIP record for this book
is available from the British Library

ISBN 978-0-571-33821-4

2 4 6 8 10 9 7 5 3 1

CONTENTS

THE FALL AT HOME

Consciousness is the turn the universe makes to hasten its own end.

§

When I am deeply jealous of someone, I perform the Buddhist practice of imagining that they are already dead: if I regard them as a passing soul, my jealousy evaporates, as I have literally nothing to be jealous of. Though I also enjoy thinking about them being dead.

§

Stopped clocks are right twice a day; clocks that run backwards, four times.

§

To a poet, a friend is just an inconvenience standing between them and a decent elegy.

§

If they told me they were beautiful, insightful or intelligent, I would agree with them. I've found it a great economy to merely reflect what others believe of themselves; besides, these things seem so little to grant anyone. But when P. declared 'I have a fine singing voice', I discovered the limit of my credulity.

Human perception is a black torch that we shine on the world to help us find things that are not there.

§

It was always my impression that mirrors do not 'double rooms'. On the contrary, they destroy rooms with their inverse, they sum the room at *almost* zero – leaving only the one thing in the real room we *can't* see. Our own face in the glass is always that of a ghost in Neverland, in Hades.

§

Nothing means anything, but what a thing *appears* to mean will tell you who is in charge.

§

Overstate one thing, mute another. No one remembers the third rule of *Fight Club.*

§

Having developed guitarist's ganglion, I looked on the web for some help, and found that 'hit it with the Bible' is still the most widely dispensed advice. What I had not foreseen was the number of the afflicted who assumed that the remedy worked by occult means, and had gone to the trouble of purchasing Bibles solely for this purpose.

A good poem should have a beginning, a middle, or an end.

§

I repeatedly found a book I intended to begin in a different room from the one in which I'd left it. On finally opening it, I realised that it had been doing its best not to read me.

§

Be wary of making an exception, lest you become that exception.

§

Between the wrong map, the broken satnav and the slumped body in the next seat, the *via negativa* was less a choice for me than a path proposed by the lack of an alternative.

§

'Now what are chances of *that*', my friend heard herself saying, as she stood on a rooftop in Brooklyn, watching the second plane slam into the tower. Oh for the bliss of a random universe.

§

We are only expressions of physical law, and therefore if *we* decide we are not without purpose – the universe is not without purpose.

The 'local delicacy' is often a tricky encounter, since it most often has its roots in making a specific poverty tolerable. Yet I knew I was in love when she took a bite of white suet pudding, and her face assumed the indescribably attractive shape of one who could not believe that something both so disgusting and delicious was allowed to be openly sold. I felt as proud as if I had cut her a slice of durian from a tree in Mindanao.

§

I read here that I write something called 'pastiche aphorisms'. In the land of the terminally ironised, one can no more prove one's sincerity than the inmate of an asylum his soundness of mind.

§

So much for free will: it appears the conscious decision to do something attaches itself *after* the unconscious has already made its choice. Even *these* words were a . . . reflex.

§

My ideal Olympics would have only the purest, most pointless games – which are also the least embarrassing, in that they have no transferable skills. What else could sustain those triathletes over their mad distances other than a silly fantasy that they are rushing to the bedside of their beloved, or fleeing death itself? What propels them over that high bar, sand-pit or hurdle but some imaginary bull or electrified fence? But race-walking, water polo, pommel horse . . . Golf! Now when the bejesus is *that* ever going to come up.

Months of hebetude, stultification, mud-brain – and suddenly, clarity, an inability to be distracted, articulate and fluent thought . . . And I immediately find myself furious with my own fickleness, or at the least the caprice of physiology to which my mind is enslaved.

§

If we *really* understood the power of taboo, we could fix everything. In a few short years, smoking in an enclosed space with strangers has become as absolute a no-no as would be exposing yourself. But the same could easily apply to money, where an air of awful fart clung stubbornly to your wads of unearned income.

§

'Truths' which turn on puns are the work of Satan, who would always have us confuse substance and shadow.

§

In so many things, what looks like talent is just the dumb patience to sit two hours longer than everyone else, staring at the patch of chaos in the page, the canvas, the score, and refusing to fill it with what will merely pass.

I am unconvinced that deep sleep or anaesthesia 'mimic death', for all that we wholly cease to identify with ourselves. (The self is merely the *identification* with a self, which is to say it is conjured in its conjuring.) But we cannot be far off reanimation; provided the memory can be frozen – from whose action alone we achieve the feat of waking as the same person each morning – we may be able to take some death-time-out; it could certainly lend some piquancy to the phrase 'gap year'. To report *what*, though? Little, other than that we awoke to the same feeling of absolute horror and dread as we did the first time.

§

If you read a poem slowly enough and carefully enough, you will find many things that are not there.

§

I was raised with the belief that one shakes off unwanted admirers by *dating* them. The Scots understand that there is often no better repellent than closer acquaintance.

§

Agnosticism is indulged only by those who have never suffered belief.

§

Science makes sense of the senseless; religion makes meaning of the meaningless.

I detest 'themed' poetry collections whose theme was not determined by personal tragedy or clinical obsession.

§

Complaining about my anthology, he accused me of 'deadism' – that is to say, I had shown too much favouritism towards the living. To which I replied that many of my best friends are dead.

§

Never afford someone who *wants* to be your enemy the pleasure of being so. Good enmities are mutually negotiated, like good relationships, then worked at, like good marriages.

§

For all her sleeplessness and worry, her ghastly childhood and violent marriage, her ill luck and her illness . . . Her beauty was untouched: her hair was thick and black, her skin taut and unblemished, and her eyes bright. All down to good genes, I suppose, but she always found it hard to command much sympathy. At least no one doubts my suffering.

It takes an almost heroic bravery to live without myth; indeed most of us are sustained by missing the point. This morning I'm thinking of that oft-repeated, heart-warming tale of how Ian Paisley and Martin McGuinness once knelt down together to pray for McGuinness's mother, a story that understandably tends to focus on neither the efficacy of prayer nor the fate of McGuinness's mother.

§

Watching a film from the 1920s. Absurd to be sad that all the children in it are now dead; yet one *always* laments the death of children, even the ancient ones.

§

I met the only living member of that golden generation last night. A charming man, but he reminded me that the last surviving Beatle is always Ringo.

§

No – the neologism is a *failure* of ingenuity. Use the damn words you have.

One small step . . . 'for a man' or 'for man'? The acoustic
analyses are perfectly inconclusive: Armstrong either omitted
the indefinite article, or elided it in the Ohioan fashion. Our
hearing the first human statement uttered from another world
as stupid or literate depends purely on what human generosity
we are inclined to extend the speaker. How exquisitely
appropriate.

§

God helps him whom God helps.

§

Truth lies in nuance. Destroy your enemy's argument not
through its countermand but its qualification.

§

Poetry isn't a calling, it's a diagnosis.

§

I gave up dreaming of revenge when I realised I could
construct no more creative torment for C. than having to wake
up as C. every morning.

An exemplary Scorpio addressed me thus: 'I don't do *direct* revenge. But I'd like to think my enemies will wake up one morning in twenty or thirty years – not devastated, not ruined . . . just a little disappointed that their lives hadn't turned out quite as well as they'd hoped.' I swear by the time he had finished speaking, the room had chilled by about ten degrees.

§

My friend has faults; my enemy, personality.

§

'Smart' isn't quite predicated on the presence of 'stupid', though I've observed that my occasional insightfulness is usually a phantasm produced by someone else's lack of it.

§

A young writer, always tweeting about his 'literary enemies' – by which, it turns out, he means those who reviewed his book badly; if only he'd realise that this confusion also explains *why*.

§

To fully grasp the oxymoron 'fellow poet', try congratulating them on their success.

Most 'inspirational quotes' attributed to great men and women are of no interest to me, being mostly precepts such as only the great can keep. One tries to write the wisdom of the fallen, such as it is.

§

Fascists hate elections but love the plebiscite, just as bullies love the show of hands.

§

The Lehman Brothers could only have existed in a world where the wicked were allowed to claim earlier precedents. The punishment for evil should be oblivion; we are condemned to repeat the past *only* if we remember it.

§

Citalopram nation. Having briefly confused myself with someone who gives a fuck, I reflect that it's amazing they didn't think to put the whole country on this stuff. Oh hang on they did. Anyway whatever.

§

Six weeks facing a wall teaches you a lot about walls, but little you can easily summarise.

I once accidentally found myself alone in the Kölner Dom after visiting hours. I had hoped the occasion would allow me to discover that it was the presence of other humans which had been standing between me and the divine; but no, it was only me.

§

Keith Jarrett once allegedly asked that the bells of Kölner Dom be silenced, as they were interfering with his rehearsal. But one permits musicians an egoism one would find a mark against any writer, where self-belief most often leads to disaster. Other than perhaps Rilke, no poet could have pulled off Scriabin's words on discovering he was about to die: 'But this is a *catastrophe!*'

§

This morning I turned over a new leaf; alas, there was a light breeze around noon.

§

A young man collars me after a reading. 'I'd like to give you this', he says, pressing a self-published pamphlet into my hand. 'Thanks' I say, stuffing it into my bag, and adding – as I always do – 'I'll read it on the train'. 'It's two quid', he says. 'That seems the right price point', I reassure him, publisher to publisher.

The outrageously successful or rich are indeed in possession of 'the secret'; but the secret is merely that, within the private confines of your own mind, there is no one but you to judge you. Shoot the co-pilot, and *do what thou wilt* truly *is* the whole of the law.

§

Her emails were discourteously long. Soon mine were discourteously short. This back-and-forth continued for some time, until I realised she thought us well matched.

§

All poets suffer from a rational fear of being understood.

§

God created us because he was lonely. Ironic, really; though I suppose he had no one to tell him that neediness is no one's most attractive quality.

§

When we checked out at forty-five, we merely died. But now we are all thanatologists.

§

If 'death is only a tragedy for the living', a true saint would make himself so loathed that no one would mourn his passing.

The failure to die at your appointed hour can only be mitigated by your silence. Alas, survival intoxicates us, and makes us garrulous.

§

One afternoon, several decades ago, I was playing badminton in a local sports hall. Following a ham-fisted and mistimed smash at the net, I sprained my ankle, and went down screaming in a kind of wheeling, one-legged Cossack dance. As I lay there poleaxed, I saw a hand reach down to help me to my feet. Through the curtain of my tears I made out the handsome, moustachioed face of Daley Thompson, then known as the world's greatest living Olympian. I can recount a largely identical story where, after playing a hideously botched guitar solo, I looked up to meet the pity-filled eyes of Sir Peter Maxwell Davis. Both occasions required me to question my atheism as no other experience had before: if *I* were God, this is *precisely* how I'd amuse myself.

§

If all you want is a book that aligns with your opinion, write it. Even better, don't.

§

'Not reaching one's full potential' need be no disaster, speaking as a failed mass murderer.

Fifty. The siesta; the waning of all activity requiring a libido; the introduction of one's prostate to the wider community; the joys of voluntarily sleeping alone; the increased awareness of how bad one's compeers and coevals often smell; the abandonment of all attempts to curb one's worst habits, following the realisation that self-improvement is most definitely not its own reward.

§

I write the things I am inclined not to say, and dream the things I am inclined not to do. I suspect those uninhibited by this protocol 'make all the difference', one way or the other.

§

It is often only the absence of dissent that alerts us to the presence of the most effective propaganda.

§

To think of oneself as a failure is to guarantee it. Others are terrified of infection, and they will swiftly quarantine you.

§

Sadder and more luminous even than those disembodied lines of Sappho's that barely consist of a sigh, that tiny scrap of the 'Trojan Iliad' discovered by Calvert Watkins, those few words of Luwian – 'when the man came down from steep Wilusa . . .' Who wouldn't die smiling, knowing *any* line of theirs would one day be read that way – dug from the blank earth, scratched on a blade of pottery, a fragment of the epic of the vanquished?

Those with no serious design on any readership beyond their own circle cannot understand *modality*, and always grant themselves the luxury of writing in a style that reflects the full range of their wit and intelligence. They will never understand that there are occasions where writing less well – or even *badly* – is the decent and correct thing to do.

§

All the more observant things I have learned about sex are too particular. By the time I am old, detached and unsexed enough to say them, they will merely disgust everyone. I suspect they will die with me, and I will not be the first.

§

The Irish boomerang: doesn't come back, but sings you a song about how much it would like to. The Scottish boomerang: doesn't come back either, but gives the impression that it *has* come back by writing Unionist op-eds for the Scottish broadsheets.

§

I wish Scots would stop complaining that the English are ruining the Highlands. Their tea is delicious and their rustic knitwear mostly excellent. Few Scots aspire to sell wholemeal muffins in Gairloch. Our exquisite revenge for Flodden was to convince the English that this is *exactly* what they wanted – to rise at five to milk the goats, while their infant children set out for school in the winter dark to learn the dying language of the Gael.

We remain most impressed with general advice, despite it being mostly impossible to take. It can *never* be summoned during those emergencies it claims to address. In this life, the golden rule has been far less use to me than 'righty-tighty, lefty-loosey'.

§

Reading Paine on theology – 'it is the study of nothing; it is founded on nothing; it rests on no principles; it proceeds by no authority; it has no data; it can demonstrate nothing; and it admits of no conclusion' – I was dismayed at having missed my calling, until I remembered *the poem*.

§

He stole your *idea*? Jesus, just steal it back.

§

My student had to the wit to attempt a *Marxist* defence of his plagiarism: all intellectual property is theft. I explained that what he had stolen was not words, but the time someone else had taken to write them; time he had now added to the stock of his own leisure.

I recall walking out of *The Cook, The Thief, The Wife & Her Lover* at an arts cinema in Brighton less because of the film's illiterate offence – sheer inertia has seen me through to the end of some of the worst movies of the age – than the company I was keeping. The liberal middle classes like to forget that, a mere twenty-five years ago, they found the sight of a woman being stabbed in the face with a fork just about the funniest thing they had ever seen, provided they could reassure themselves that the context was sufficiently ironised. They were a herd, no less good or bad than any other herd.

§

In the name of the 'balanced account' we now see the central weighed against the fringe, the informed against the ignorant, the scientific against the magical, the good against the evil. A reminder that we will be destroyed not by the *absence* of justice or democracy, but by their perversion.

§

The lie of why. Karma is merely reminding ourselves that nothing follows because it's deserved or earned, or because it must punish or reward us . . . The Law does not take that level of interest in our fates. All follows simply because it follows, and ignorance is the mere denial of a universe whose governing principle is flow, however much we like to think of it as 'consequence'.

Heroes last only as long as their arenas. What of those titans of discontinued sports – all the distance plungers, one-handed weightlifters, standing jumpers, and live pigeon shooters of yesteryear? What of Ray Ewry? And when we decide that *war* is a ludicrous recreation . . . Achilles himself will be incomprehensible, and then forgotten.

§

The stars used to mean the *limit* of our knowledge, for which our gratitude was infinite.

§

In the delay between cause and effect we introduce the idea of fate, mainly through our impatience.

§

She saw through everyone, until they had all gone.

§

I dread 'men and women of principle'. The clue is in the singular. Most damage is done through compromising the smaller decencies in the name of one great dumb belief.

§

I expect economics to be revealed one day as an occult science, i.e. one which creates the reality it then investigates.

'His survivors include his wife of 31 years.' Strange this turn of phrase should apply only to the deceased; I know several women who would claim to have survived me.

§

People would understand their own zombification if they had a better understanding of what constitutes a *word*. Speech is lexicalised whenever we already know the meaning of a phrase. In the course of our reflexive twitter, longer and longer phrases are turned to stone; whole conversations are conducted in which not one word is consciously improvised, and are nothing but stock phrases sewn together in half-sleep.

§

Neomanagerialism: the present cult of all our institutions, where The Form has dispensed with the need for trust between agents. Form-filling busywork, they tell us, will make us free, and is an intrinsic moral good. Why? Because we are dictated to by middle management, and the powerful always valorise their own expertise: were we ruled by janitors, there would be hourly fire drills and I would be obliged to give lectures carrying a bucket of sawdust. Now, we do little but make preparations for a thousand imaginary legal and procedural challenges, none of which ever come to pass; but we are ready, always ready, with our paper trails, our feedback sheets, our detailed reports and testimonies, all generated at great professional inconvenience – and which no one, absolutely *no one*, ever reads. [See: *The Fall of Rome*.]

There are two kinds of *true* enemies: those we secretly love, as they remind us of ourselves; and those who body forth the monsters we would have become, had we not mastered ourselves. As for the others . . . We can sustain little real interest in them.

§

Again and again, he insults me in the press, in his academic papers, on his Twitter account, within direct earshot . . . Again and again, he expects me to behave with nothing but decorous courtesy when we meet face to face. And I always oblige him, leaving him tormented by the thought that he will never discover the form of my revenge.

§

A long interview with Borges at 80, conducted by a man who has deluded himself that he is the old man's peer; he hogs the conversation with his own sesquipedalian prattle, and occasionally condescends to ask something which he thinks shows his biting insight. Borges, who had perfected his routine of exaggerated diplomacy decades before, answers his interlocutor with meticulous courtesy, respectfully consults his opinion, and reserves his polite demurral only for the more unforgivable of his idiocies. It took me a while to realise that, of course, *Borges* was conducting the interview, and just paying out the rope.

§

One must take writing seriously enough to sometimes *stop*, perhaps for good. Those who have never seriously considered the possibility are usually writers by choice, not birth.

That's all very well, but were I *actually* to 'live every day as if it were my last', right now I'd be lying on the floor with my hands in my pants and my mouth open under a Mr Whippy machine, waiting for the police to show up and arrest me for the murder of Boris Johnson.

§

Poets: if it already *has* a name, stop bothering it.

§

Apart from anything else, not knowing the hour of one's death is a disaster for sensible time management: I watch Netflix like an immortal.

§

Never trust the optimism of optimists.

§

My shrink's refrain: 'everyone is always doing their best'. Yes, I understand the broad principle. But what troubles me is that – if it's true – that means everyone but *me*.

What passes for fine writing these days is mere fluency in cliché; what disguises the fact is a failure to grasp that cliché is a disease of degree. 'Well done!' our creative writing teachers say, 'I have heard all these phrases somewhere before, and you have succeeded in presenting me with a plausible simulacrum of a piece of literature, free from the terrors of a single original phrase or idea which might provoke my actual engagement, or demand my actual attention.' When *everyone* is a writer, 'the high style' must be redefined as something to which everyone feels they could reasonably aspire.

§

Poetry is *always* a struggle to read; therefore no one should have any interest in any poem which didn't half kill its author.

§

The evening before the flight: the too-familiar hysterics, *precisely* as intense as last time . . . My miraculous survival of all my other airborne experiences providing me with nothing but a sense of my own dwindling luck. A present lived entirely in the future, and so perfectly focussed on one event that *when* the moment arrives, when one *actually* steps right-foot-first aboard the floating box – it feels as if 'one's time has come', whatever that means, and that this the only time that has ever truly existed: I am *always* on the damn plane.

§

To win most arguments – establish that which your opponent regards as an intrinsic property. Invariably, it will not be.

Nothing can *be* without the real possibility that it cannot be; it must be existentially falsifiable. The formulation 'but if there is nothing which cannot exist – then nothing itself can exist' just makes the silly error of mistaking nothing for something, a reification perhaps necessary to appreciate *anything*.

§

I drink to forget about money.

§

Picabia: *Les explications mystiques sont les plus superficielles.* Always prefer even a *bad* material explanation than one predicated on fairies.

§

Poet: one who can sit down to write in the fullness of the dawn as if it was the stroke of midnight.

§

Agent: one who will immediately vouch for the brilliance of your new book without having read a word of it.

§

Publisher: despite their reputation, the only angels of literature; we are the unacknowledged mitigators of human shame.

Predictably, he named our great radical experimentalist as his favourite poet. His eyes glistened with *love*. What's your favourite line of his? I asked. He could not recall one. OK, what's your favourite *poem* of his? His work was too even in its brilliance to choose. *This* merit, it was clear, was why X was their favourite: his poetry was not disrupted by the merest whisper of a memorable effect, which would have destroyed the immaculate consistency of the whole. Our gods must be admired *in toto*.

§

I am not sure that your poem effortlessly surviving its translation pays it much of a compliment.

§

Wisdom is an act; stupidity is a condition.

§

I decided to bury the hatchet, and the back of his head seemed as good a place as any.

§

You are quite wrong to read into my disparagement of everyone else's poetry any high opinion of my own. Worms have no king or kingdom.

I keep setting goals, when what I really want is the road towards them; I wish merely to be *goal-orientated*. I recall my grandfather's bleak Calvinist advice: 'always walk as if you're going somewhere'. I guess.

§

A piece of accidentally sentient dirt, a saprophyte that shook off its root and stem and learned to forage.

§

If I really have to 'learn how to love myself before I can learn how to love you', then you can fuck off.

§

If you don't want your entire oeuvre to be represented by your worst poem: don't write it.

§

Selfwork in one's fifties: forcing yourself to be hungry when you want to be sated, wake when you want to be asleep, mobile when you want to remain still, present when you would rather be absent.

When I used to call myself a 'feminist', I would absolve myself of any vigilance towards my own behaviour; I stopped, and started calling myself 'a supporter of the feminist movement'. It was the same when I was a 'person of faith'. *Any* soi-disanterie means crediting oneself with intrinsic qualities: one's virtue or sin is a settled matter, and not something to be questioned, least of all by oneself.

§

Is it just me, or do other folk have no problem with the particle-wave function? I too am neither here nor there unless observed.

§

Understandably, no one ever comments on the *pathos* of the end of empires, since only another empire could possibly sympathise.

§

The 'smartphone', that clam of hell, that Claude glass of the age, that rear-view mirror that will one day be filled with the clear blue heavens as we stumble over the cliff-edge with the wind whistling in our ears.

§

The most noble reason to write a biography is to deter an autobiographer.

In middle age, I find it harder and harder to keep any company at all. The young say nothing you don't already know; the old, nothing you want to hear; your coevals have nothing to say anyway, and like you are trapped between nostalgia and dread.

§

I once had a nuisance caller, but took to just setting down the phone so their bill could mount while I hoovered or cooked or listened to the radio. The better revenge is not just to cease to care what an enemy thinks of you – they must also *know* this, so that their anger turns inward.

§

No one laughs alone without their face unconsciously relaxing into a slightly sadder expression than it had worn before.

§

I know of no poet who survived either unexpected wealth, psychoanalysis or enlightenment.

Those empty weeks spent in some remote Highland fastness, pencils sharpened and 'notebook' open, before a window framing perfect scenery . . . All I did was stare into the middle distance and drink. And today, with the dregs of a migraine, crammed into a corner on a shitty commuter train to Basel, I get more decent work done in twenty minutes typing with one thumb into a phone than I did all last month, without feeling a flicker of inspiration at any point. Inspiration is our occasional and incidental *reward* for good work, whose source is really something far more mysterious and haphazard.

§

Contentment. Odd to aspire to a thing I have seen in its most refined form only in morons or late-stage dementia patients. Peace, rather; a nobler goal, given that it can only be wrought from discord.

§

Good style is removing every unnecessary word, bar one.

§

Our rare 'bursts of inspiration' have given spontaneity an undeservedly good name.

I have often been in the company of writers who, mid-conversation, will take their notebook from their jacket to *jot something down.* Only the torpor that invariably accompanies my contempt stopped me from strangling them on the spot.

§

I can be flattered into doing anything, however wicked, and cajoled out of my worst behaviour by an unflattering comparison. I am no one, and whoever discovers this owns me.

§

Those poets – I am one such – whose favourite words are 'ruin', 'desolate', 'derelict', 'bedlam', 'nothing', 'shambles', 'dismantle', 'abandoned', 'lost' . . . They are the worst Romantics, or the best, there being absolutely no difference. Failures even in failing, they are in love with the idea of their own fall, while avoiding the reality of it at all costs. (Genuine fallers are all ecstasy, or all screaming.)

§

I have spent far too much time wondering how the singularity felt just before it exploded. My current theory is 'intolerably itchy'. All this, for want of a scratch.

§

Speak in public as if you were being simultaneously translated.

In my mind, I am always on the point of being fired, or demoted to the lowest rank through some unforgivable administrative blunder, accidental indiscretion or obscure breach of protocol, always treating junior colleagues as if they were my senior – all long past the point this might have served to 'keep me grounded'. But if I did not constantly make myself a omega male, I would have no rage, no grievance, no reason to pump myself up for . . . *this*?

§

Poetry is the corner language is finally backed into when surrounded by the wolves of reality. But sometimes it will conjure a real torch from thin air.

§

We forget – until perhaps our deathbeds – that words like 'accomplishment' and 'achievement' are merely metaphors, and that we incarnate, sum, and possess nothing.

§

'Liar' and 'lyre' are more than homophones.

§

As my mother still tells me, the word 'sorry' will be on my gravestone. Indeed my love of apologies preceded my sins, and probably inspired most of them.

Death structures time as mass structures space: subtly, at a distance; but were you to stand on its cratered surface, you could not tell apart at the ticking and the chime.

§

The sight of a young couple in love fills me with joy and good wishes; a happily married young couple, the keen anticipation of their ruin.

§

For me to now marry would be like converting to Catholicism: I would have to do so for mystical reasons alone.

§

Last night I dreamt of the circus. All the clowns and lions and acrobats and little trained monkeys gathered round a puppy, which they then tore to pieces. The children were delighted, and crying with laughter.

§

I used to believe that 'the goal' was to see reality stripped of all human illusion; and I recall the afternoon I managed to do so, for maybe four or five minutes. To this day I am haunted by the chaotic hell I witnessed.

Thank God I can barely drink these days, and have never learned to touch-type. These are the only two things standing between me and *the work of fiction*.

§

Don't mistake my despair for *mere* despair; it has purpose. From this well, I can see the stars at noon.

§

I wish I had committed a single positive act as powerfully alive and vivid in the memory as any one of my public humiliations.

§

Those delicious mornings when one wakes and has not yet remembered *not to be evil*, when one could start a cult before breakfast.

§

I remember to be present only when I forget my 'goal'.

§

The presence of art is the absence of the beholder.

Most human relationships founder because people give what gives them *pleasure* to give, or give that which they themselves most value; but to give what is actually needed is often difficult, boring, costly, or apparently pointless. She wanted your time, not your love; he wanted your touch, not your encouragement; she wanted your support, not your advice; he needed your money, not your gift.

§

Thanks to us, the dog is only now half an animal. Mercifully, the other half is the best part of a human.

§

Gods lend the void a hierarchy.

§

First day of solo living after thirty years. I meet myself in the hall coming back from the kitchen, and to my dismay I see we now have no way of avoiding each other.

§

My recovery from the light takes longer and longer; I can see the time when I will require nothing less than the darkness between lifetimes.

Condemned to the perspective of the living, with their fixed POV and goddamned 'internal life'.

§

Nothing wrong with material possession if it creates a spiritual enhancement. A new hi-fi system, an even bigger television . . . All these things might conceivably 'enrich' my enjoyment of, say, Mompou or Scorsese. But the trouble is there is nothing we *want* which we won't find a way to admit into this category.

§

Now I was living alone again, I resolved that I would stop furnishing rooms in order to impress the important guests I neither invited nor desired. I would instead construct a home wholly to my own taste and habits. After briefly contemplating the installation of a TV in the bathroom, a trough in the kitchen and the conversion of the spare room into a masturbatorium, I decided to revert to my old strategy, since it was clearly the only thing keeping me from the dung-heap.

§

Drugs – or at least the cocktail of opiates and adrenaline suppressants that shape my day – have taught me something I would never have believed as a younger man: that one might escape actually *dying*, and instead reduce oneself to nothing by degrees.

Our idiocy in making love transitive, in thinking it a *solution* to anything.

§

I recall, from my twenties, an attic room, a skylight full of sky, and glossing her back with my tongue from brainstem to asshole and back again – and somewhere within that fluent circuit learning all I cared to take away from this life.

§

The last human would be like the last word: meaningless, and nothing without their dictionary of other souls.

§

I resolve to write a few lines every night, just after my 3 am piss, since it's then I'm most disembodied, i.e. least acquainted with myself. I soon give up. I *forget* to – or if I do remember, find myself immaculately indifferent to the whole project. I had mistakenly thought of my state as a detachment of the self, but at that hour I have no self at all. The self does not 'sleep': all the soul *is* is its own awakening. Nor does it 'die' when we sleep. We cease to identify with it; and therefore its existence becomes an academic matter.

§

When you say you love me, you think you're paying me a compliment; I think you're slandering yourself.

The universal enhancers: low light, alcohol, hats, the act of singing well, the face in orgasm, a sense of humour, intelligence, power, money . . . As for 'the look of love', that all depends.

§

Close but no cigar. Pace Shelley: weep not for the future, fear not for the past. *Pace* Berra: sometimes it's over before it's over. *Pace* Freud: sometime a penis really is just a penis.

§

Nothing worse than some fucker with a plan.

§

I have noticed that those who have known coma-time are very bad at getting back to you with any urgency, and seem to know something we don't.

§

Blair thought his best defence his *sincerity*; a quality I never doubted – but how did the idea arise that wicked men must have wicked intentions?

The aphorism, like the feedback questionnaire, is also a form of anonymous response. So, for the record, dear students – you, young sir, who feels my marking disgracefully harsh, or you, miss, who thinks I should self-censor (given as I am to 'irrelevant and extreme left-wing outbursts every two minutes'): I have altered my behaviour not a jot in the light of your comments, and indeed am resolved to redouble my efforts in future. And just as you would the authorship of your remarks, I will deny the sincerity of mine, if challenged by my employers.

§

I simplify people to their outward form, to their 'dealings', the way I simplify countries to their coasts and borders. And just so, I hope they gain little sense of my own redneck flyover states, the goat-centric, feudal villages of my central Turkey . . .

§

We should never forget that writing has its origins in the issuing of receipts, and the recording of debt. Every word is also a secret reckoning.

§

Anyone whose students 'teach him as much as he teaches them' should lose half his salary.

§

I can tell from my dog that pain came before anguish, which is to say anguish is a hobby of mine.

I travel frequently, and treat silence as a kind of pop-up temple: I wear two pairs of noise-cancelling headphones, one on top of the other. I have experimented with the simultaneous closing down of other senses too, with blindfolds, and with drugs which render me insensate. But in the end, the internal racket increases: the whispering needle of my tinnitus, the lorry-traffic of the blood, the removal men of the heart, the random fireworks of my retinal phosphenes, the wretched experimental European cinema of my unconscious . . . It all serves merely to isolate the great dark auditorium of the body, where one can focus on every twinge and twang, buzz and ache it can produce. There are no real retreats but death and distraction.

§

'Only God can be an atheist'? Only a god without an ego, which seems, frankly, a stretch.

§

Nothing infuriates us more than the inability to find fault with someone we loathe. Bad matches with assholes tend to last far longer than bad matches with saints.

§

'But it's really important to show the *process*', the film-maker whined, turning the camera to the mirror once again. Indeed he broke the fourth wall so often one suspected it of having ruined his childhood.

I suspect my ability to find *all* women in some way attractive is a form of misogyny, but I still await a convincing explanation as to why.

§

Anti-theism is more honourable than mere atheism: that you find gods *abhorrent* is a moral position.

§

My only explanation as to why I failed to offer a word of comfort to my dying friend was that I needed at that time to think as little of myself as possible, and she presented me with a golden opportunity.

§

Disaster bears down upon us like a roaring juggernaut, and yet we insist on reading omens in the water and the wind, and require that the birds give us their little signs.

§

A significant component of beauty is its absolute indifference towards me.

§

For a non-poet to make a poetic translation is like a non-driver climbing into the cockpit of a plane in the hope their luck will somehow improve.

Death makes us metronomes.

§

Sometimes, yes, poetry is 'lost in translation'; more often it seems to have been kidnapped from the street, flown to a black site and then tortured into silence or derangement. The default mode of all non-anglophone poets surely *cannot* be a straight choice between banality and surrealism.

§

He wrote to me at my work address, specifically to tell me he found my book deplorable. Seventy-three, playing the bongos and the recorder with a free jazz ensemble, firing out incomprehensible haiku in numbered letterpress runs of forty, his anger and offence undiminished and apparently inexhaustible . . . I am as in love with the avant-garde as I was at fifteen. To *liberate* oneself from the audience!

§

Most jazz musicians suffer from instrument envy, and this fuels a great deal of technical innovation; likewise poets with languages not their own.

The male artist becomes not his father but his *mentor*. I was mistaken for him the other day: bald, white-bearded, round-shouldered, rather deliberately 'cutting a miserable figure' as I bought a tin of old-man soup. I might have chosen more carefully at the time, but he, it transpired, was the shape of my ambition.

§

Reputation, I have calculated, travels at the rate of fifty miles a year, and I am now represented in American anthologies by my juvenilia.

§

Satan converses in the language of publisher's blurbs, and I speak as his amanuensis.

§

Many years ago, an encounter with an older, wiser writer: we were drunk at a tequila party and both clearly contemplating the practicalities and consequences of a fuck in the toilets. I managed to hold her gaze for far longer than I might have dared sober. 'Christ', she said. 'You really *do* believe the eyes are the windows to the soul.' Never had youth been so aware of its own callowness.

§

A poet reveals his sources even more reluctantly than a journalist, but only because they would instantly discredit him.

Lied to constantly throughout her childhood about the actual hell of her daily existence, she had worked thereafter to free herself of all illusion, and with total success. Illusion was then reasonably denied to all those whom she loved: no motive was allowed to go unexamined, no generous act allowed to stand without a comment on its hidden venality or self-interes. . . . The world became *exactly* as intolerable as it really is. I understand and admire the caustic purity of her vision. My childhood, however, was a bliss; therefore as an adult I do not share her need for reality.

§

Sometimes I understand that this world is a simulacrum, like those sparkling little Canadian tourist towns that appear to have been delivered flat-pack, half an hour before your arrival. Not a stage-set; just a fake, a flimsy premise, a show house, a conceit in which no one can really be at home.

§

Should God be inclined to make himself *known* to me, he should be made very welcome; but I have better things to do than play 'hunt the omnipresent'.

§

The evil act is just a miracle in reverse; both are 'inexplicable' only through our refusal to seek an explanation.

Through my decent ecclesiastical connections I had secured
a good seat in the corner of the choir at evensong. I had risen
very early that morning and forgone my 3 p.m. shut-eye, and
was a little woozy. As evensongs go, it was pleasant enough,
though it did little to command my wakeful attention. The
visiting Dutch choir was decent but unexceptional, the lesson
some absurd passage of Old Testament bingo – the Lord this,
Jerusalem that, begat this, smite that. I then remembered
something I'd done recently, involving a scorecard, an injured
fox and a rushed escape from a building under siege, the whole
episode a little pointless in its direction, and with more than
the hint of the nonsensical about it . . . Though I could not for
the life of me remember how the story had ended. Then one
after another – ten, twelve, fifteen such memories ran to the
front of my mind; they were so strange that I assumed they
must be fragments of all the forgotten dreams I'd had over
the last couple of months. They came in a rush, like those
revolving-door moments of déjà vu, unravelling the solidity
of the present (I assume it was a panic attack of some kind; I
was falling in love at the time). And at the thought of my mind
brimming, spilling, then constantly refilling with this garbage
of its own creation . . . I prayed there and then for it to be
immediately *flushed out*. Heaven is the oubliette of the eternal
now.

§

When I experience those moments of the eternal, I re-enter
my childhood: that infinity of distinct yet wholly inarticulable
states, which the acquisition of speech and concept cut to a
miserable fraction. But I could once see a million colours.

Bad news demands a straight delivery in proportion to its severity. 'I'm fine, thank you – now you said you had some news about my entire family?'

§

When at 16 I renounced my faith and absolved myself of sin, I saw quickly that I could also absolve myself of a redeemer – and for the first time, actually *felt* Christ's sorrow, albeit only for the hollowness of his own sacrifice.

§

Everything passes, and consciousness is its only impediment.

§

She looked radiant, and when I asked her her secret, she told me it was because she could not sleep. It had the odd effect of making her eyes brighter, her skin lucent and taut, and conferred upon her an uncannily wired and attentive aura. 'But *I* can't sleep!' I yelled, pointing with some justified indignation to my own face. 'Yes,' she snapped, 'but for *different reasons.*'

§

My fear of fucking up has no effect whatsoever on my ability to fuck up; on the contrary, it means I spend my time in meticulous rehearsal.

A good bishop I know had just conducted a huge crowd in a city square in a minute's silence; in relating this fact he could not keep the glint of despotic ecstasy from his eyes.

§

Vanities. I receive a request from a festival for a publicity photo, and send the same one I have used for ten years, taken during the week I was going to the gym. When I arrive, the festival director looks down at the picture in the brochure, then looks at me, and asks in a grave and solicitous whisper *Have you been very ill?* Drunk on the plane coming home, I proudly show the stranger next to me a picture of my children. She looks at the photo, then looks at me, and says: *their mother must be very beautiful.*

§

I have no patience with the unpunctual. Time is the only real thing I own.

§

She discovered her true genre was the deathbed speech, and was thereafter in no hurry to leave us.

§

Only the shamelessly ambitious can deal with success with any grace. If you want to see a saint spoil, curdle, rot from within – give them a prize for 'best saint'.

Post hoc ergo propter hoc is chiselled on the tombstone of the race, still insisting it died of natural causes.

§

Even in Kyoto, Basho longed for Kyoto; but Basho could not have known that we *all* long for Kyoto.

§

My happiness or misery are adult constructions, in that they required me to stand back and appraise my state. As a small child I was unaware of either, and I *was* my feelings.

§

Having three relationships to increase the love in your life is like wearing three watches to buy time.

§

To heal without a scar is a waste of a good wound.

§

'I didn't ask to be born!' howled my son, just as I had at the same age. I did not explain that I'd declined to further the cause of those who *did* ask, figuring his general indifference made him a far safer addition to humanity.

What I miss most about smoking is the *fire*, having our most alien element so close to my face every moment of the day.

§

S., presumably thinking it makes his house *welcoming,* has chairs lined up in his hall, stuffed into his porch, his parlour, his stair landing – even though he lives alone. But chairs invite tired ghosts, and his whole house was like a waiting room by the Acheron.

§

On his deathbed, he requested that we forget him. What a vanity to imagine that I'd go to *that* kind of trouble.

§

Genius: half intelligence, half disinhibition, and half excess.

§

M. was always a great one for 'the imaginative leap', even when all that was required is the littlest step.

§

I can think of no monster whose life, on closer examination, does not compel our sympathy. However there are occasions where the moral thing to do is to resist that examination.

There is no collective noun for poets: they all refuse one. A uniqueness of poet.

§

Snakes cast the least shadow.

§

The journey; the dream; the wakening 'between' two eternities ... No, we're soap bubbles – a sphere of mind bounded by an opalescent film of selfhood, blown into being by the mere agitation of the elements, like the spume on the sea, a sea to which we will not even know we have returned.

§

'Ambient semantics' is the poetic mode du jour. If a poem merely *feels* like it might mean something, if its images are pregnant with symbolic *intent* . . .

§

Poetry: a fear of the right margin.

§

Those lucky artists born with a powerful noun in their name, or who had the wit to adopt such a name early in their careers. Good or bad, they easily assume the *brand*. I have left it too late to change my name to Jeff Cataclysm, and regret it bitterly.

[51]

Sentimentality is the art of empathising with oneself.

§

And even in the country of the two-eyed, the one-eyed man still has better aim.

§

One mostly flogs a dead horse out of love.

§

In the end, I embraced the death of my imagination much in the way Peter Abelard did his castration: one might as well turn a misfortune into a virtue, into – to hell with it – an aspect of one's *appeal.* Look at me! I am now a man wholly undistracted from his task, whatever it was.

§

Working at a relationship might keep it seaworthy, but salvaging is for shipwrecks.

§

Genius flowers by different means. Knowing he was Miles Davis made all the difference in the world to Miles Davis. But Bill Evans was Bill Evans largely on account of him *not* realising he was Bill Evans. The disadvantage with the second approach is that people like Bill Evans cannot wait to die, and barely care if all their tunes are stolen.

There is no easier role than being 'ahead of one's time', since it remains to be seen if any time will transpire in which one makes any sense. Far more difficult is being in *step* with one's time, which requires a horrific intimacy with it.

§

That 'the poor always require a subspecies' is a cliché the educated wealthy classes privately dismiss as an excuse for a moral failing; but what would these half-wit expendables know?

§

R. pre-empts and makes meticulous 'full disclosures' before every book review: the publisher is currently looking at his manuscript; Y is a slight acquaintance; X once bought him a drink; Z's sister once shared a cupcake with him . . . Indeed I have never encountered a critic more certain of his own corruptibility.

§

What is experienced once as eternal by definition remains eternal. And if we increase our store of such moments, we increase the extent to which our lives are braided with eternity.

People seem untroubled that Socrates' reasoning was quite circular: all he said, after he drank the hemlock, was that he was learning that tune on the flute because he wanted to learn that tune on the flute. It could be, I'll concede, that 'the goal of knowledge is knowledge itself'; but it's just as likely that he really liked learning stuff on the flute, and saw no reason to stop in the last five minutes. Keep eating, keep painting, keep masturbating, keep learning; for the only goal is to know – finally, with perfect clarity and with no rancour – that there *is* no goal; which is what Socrates was really teaching us.

§

The quickest way to fix a spiritual crisis is to absolve oneself of a soul.

§

The French seem to have a special case called the 'absolutive' reserved for the intellectual novelty. Not for them the qualified utterance; it's the void or nothing.

§

To remind oneself how small one is in universal terms is salutary, but usually accompanied by the urge to do absolutely nothing, since nothing we do can have much consequence – or to do something completely insane, for much the same reason. For better or worse, we have to cultivate a fake sense of proportion, and confine our acts to the human scale.

Those little walking certitudes, those accelerationists and neo-Randians – the last human sentimentality is not 'a failure to hand ourselves over to the natural forces of technocapitalism': it is to continue to indulge the opinions of those least representative of the species. Jail them, or banish them all. I would far rather humanity died for the conscience it briefly kept alive.

§

Power is never won without the terror of its loss; hence the dynasty.

§

I go to sleep conscientiously thinking about sex, or working out some intervallic study on the guitar, or shooting a game of 9-ball – principally as these are the aspects of the physical world I can eidetically summon, almost as if am afraid to let that world go. But increasingly I find that I have internalised the dead too, and can converse with them; those we have loved we memorise. We can *remember* the living, but (infatuated love excepted) we don't create them within us, as there's yet no need. Besides, the dead talk to us of very different things, in their infinite leisure, and their total absence of fear.

§

Those who do not learn to imitate die of feeling.

I look to the past to remember who I am, and work towards the future to know who I will be, and between the two I forget to exist.

§

By definition, 'meaning' is the one word we have to define from scratch every time we use it; it's the black hole around which our galaxy of signs rotates, and of which we ideally would never speak.

§

Minor talents can still be the brief avatars of real gods – but the gods pass through them quickly, and not without much tearing from their hooks.

§

Failures all dream of success; but what's less appreciated is that the successful often dream of failure, whose romance they have been denied. Not for them the nobility of going towards the grave, invisible, misjudged and misunderstood. No, they have been understood all too well, and fed past satiety.

§

Never accept or reject a compliment. If you reject it, you have made an immediate enemy; if you accept it, a future one. Instead deflect the praise, and turn it gently to the handsome venue, the receptive audience, the talented couturier, the pleasant weather – or best of all, to the flatterer, who will be quite unprepared for the early return of their demon.

Age teaches us that we don't have the leisure to resist the obvious conclusion. That Free Church of Scotland minister in Uist, was it? who first translated the *Odyssey* into Gaelic but declined to publish it, as Man had need of only one book. The first time I heard this story, I was inclined to see in it the kind of rabbinical paradox Jabès would have delighted in: yes, we know about the exquisite self-inscription of failure that comes with all human enterprise, but few have the clarity of mind to perform such a *pre-emptive* act of self-defeat. But the other day I thought of this story again, and realised the man was just a damn clown.

§

Another day as a professional sparer of blushes, a fixer of bad lines, when one realises one has amounted to no more than 'one who had seen through poetry' . . .

§

She called me from the morgue to assure me. 'Yep: he's definitely dead.' 'How does he look?' 'Exactly like himself, minus himself.'

§

Any advice that begins with 'He who . . .' has already lost me: on a point of principle, I am *never* that guy.

§

Some critics hate your work; others hate you – but none are more vicious than those who once held out the highest hopes for you.

Most of the 'self-sacrifice' one hears of involves little that has not been renounced with ease. Far more of ourselves is denied in the most venal of our pursuits.

§

In being born and so *quickly* learning of our fate, we are 'the done for'. Not a bad epithet for the species.

§

You don't know what you've lost till you've got it back.

§

Bizarre that we treat our approaching non-existence as the exceptional event, when it's so clearly *life*.

§

He was raised with nothing, and now he wanted everything. And *goddamn* if he wasn't going to do absolutely nothing to get it.

§

The born again: the ultimate gluttons for punishment.

A poem has to do something very paradoxical: transport the heaviest freight, by *air*. But I have no interest in those contraptions which, after some obscene display of urgency, barely manage to claw themselves into the sky. I want an anti-gravity machine made from gyroscopes, one that lifts gently from the ground until it purrs into the clouds.

§

How much wisdom was ruined by a lousy rhyme? And how many lies were believed because of a good one?

§

I preferred not to think that no one had come, but rather that my reading was being held in total secrecy.

§

A student brings me a Xerox of a page of *Henderson the Rain King,* with most of the words whited out to reveal what I assume was a poem. 'What's this?' I ask. 'It's an "erasure" poem', he replies. I tell him it's half-finished. The remark passes over him, silently and very high, like the Hubble telescope. I have a loathing of all art made *procedurally*, which makes me want to smash it for the mere sake of introducing into it some minimal human warmth.

In my dreams of afterlives and other universes, I don't fear a wrathful creator, nor a recreationally wicked demon; in time, these might be placated, reasoned with, tricked . . . No. The real horror is that there is *nothing taking an interest in any of this*, and that there is only mere statistical chaos.

§

The idea that Poetry and Reason are inimical seems to have been put about solely by Poetry.

§

No, 'words are not things in themselves'. But reassuringly neither are things.

§

I gather Thomas Merton had a document from the Vatican confirming his status as 'hermit'. What a fine thing to show any visitor one tires of, mid-dessert!

§

Society denies its Neros until the last minute. Their spectacle beguiles us, until all the fires are lit.

§

Every plague rat has a moment when he thinks he has subjugated his realm when he has merely consumed it.

I once asked a free climber how on earth she could cling to the sheer rockface for so long, in such agonised, contorted shapes as her few hand- and footholds dictated. She said, 'Oh, it's not the muscle that holds the pose – it's the skeleton.' I there and then resolved to allow that part of me which is *already* dead to take more of the strain.

THE BLIND EYE

As a native Damascene, all my revelations came on the road to elsewhere. All were eclipses, all were skies falling silent.

§

The male genitals are worn externally as evolution is in the process of expelling them from the body. Another million years and they'll be stored in a drawer.

§

I can see exactly what *not* to do at the moment. No doubt through the usual process of elimination I'll arrive at my favourite strategy of total paralysis.

§

Ego-surfing again, four months since I last dared: the hit-count tripled, nearly all of them namechecks by brand-new enemies, or recruits to the army of doppelgängers – champion disco-dancers, Alaskan Romanticists, men who teach juggling, fuck donkeys, or put miniature combine harvesters in bottles . . . Of whom I would have known nothing, if vanity hadn't tricked me into putting my head round this mirrored corridor of hell again. Good that at least one of our sins now carries its immediate terrestrial punishment.

Everything is driven towards entropy, and yet everywhere aspires to the order still inscribed in it by our primal singularity, our cosmic egg – and falls into sphere, orbit, season and pulse. But how sad to find yourself born into a universe founded on the principle of *nostalgia*.

§

With your back to the wall, always pay a compliment. Even your mugger or torturer is not immune to flattery, and still capable of being a little disarmed by a word of congratulation on their choice of footwear or superior technique.

§

I wonder if anyone was ever tempted to play a trick on Helen Keller, and communicate to her that she was really dead. Then again, I once played the same trick on myself, and have done nothing but seek my minute-by-minute reassurance from everything since. This is why I touch everyone all the time; you will see me display the same overfamiliarity towards the furniture.

§

Whale to the ocean, bird to the sky, man to his dream.

In hell, the Postmoderns are awarded a huge, sensitive and critically informed general readership. I wish them sales; I wish them the *book group* . . .

§

No sense steps into the same word twice.

§

The Calvinist knife-edge. Self-loathing gets me out of bed in the morning; but for years it kept me in it.

§

The aphorism: too much too soon or too little too late, but never just enough for the time being.

§

After a reading in Rotterdam, a woman came up to me and complimented me on my performance. I half-heard her, and made her repeat what she had just said. 'Sorry!' I replied, 'I just wanted to hear you say it twice . . .' My weak little joke was either lost on her, or somehow fatally misjudged; she threw up her hands in despair and stormed off. 'I can now turn on a sixpence,' I thought to myself, 'compress the effect of several years of my acquaintance into a matter of *seconds* . . .'

Poetry! What a fine thing to be working in a medium that brings out the best only in the murderous soul of the poet, and quite the very worst in everyone else. Even a limerick will dig out the one grain of ugly ambition in the heart of a saint.

§

When I was ill, I could hear the rhythmic ictus in all conversation, as clear as a snare drum; I was as aware of the speed of the car as if the road were an inch from my own outstretched fingertips; I saw how my every human exchange took place without my conscious volition. In other words: I lost all sense of unreality.

§

Most worrying was his new habit of referring to himself in the third person plural.

§

I realise whatever minimal physical appeal I may once have possessed has long faded, but I should have put more store by it at the time: I foolishly believed I might rely on my personality a little longer.

§

The smartest operators cultivate the young. Our contemporaries are least able – and least inclined – to guarantee our futures.

The song was going so well, until I heard him *express himself* ... Then I knew I could never play it again, as I'd spend all my time in anticipatory dread of that one note.

§

His friendship was index-linked to my popularity, and would cool and warm and cool again over the course of a single evening. After one fortuitous but rather spectacular witticism, he offered me the use of his villa in the Turks and Caicos. Alas, I was fatally emboldened by this small success, and by the time the coffee arrived he had forgotten my name again.

§

Despite taking the Buddha's advice on these matters – 'when you commit a slander, imagine your mouth filled with excrement' – my casual perfidy never fails to astonish me. They will never buy my best defence, which is that it was purely *recreational* ...

§

In the arts, mere reflection does for epiphany among the poor. A smash-hit piece of local theatre might consist of little more than a public recitation of their street names and council estates.

§

Sixty years old, and still a paragon of hip insouciance. Still without the courage to fail, even a little.

He spent his life paralysed by imaginary protocols.

§

In purgatory, we're shown how narrow were the opportunities
we missed; in hell, how narrow were those we took; and in
heaven, that nothing could have been otherwise.

§

Sex is better in dreams as the prick has an eye.

§

An afternoon watching the Paralympics, the 100m butterfly
won by a swimmer with no arms, head-butting the end of the
pool in order to finish. An astonishing performance I was on
my feet to applaud; though to my shame I found there was a
part of me also wishing that the human spirit would sometimes
triumph just a little *less*.

It is not the sophistication but the poverty of a people that is revealed by the local flourishes of their speech. The infinite Sami terms for snow, the eighty shades of green a Nepali can summon by name, are really just the songs of thin economies, which *always* demand this kind of fine discrimination and hyponymic explosion – and are beautiful only to the alien eavesdropper. Scots, for example, has sixty-three words for different kinds of expectoration, being simply our traditional impediment to work. *Kechle, kisty-whistle* and *black hoast* may even sound charming to you; to me they do little more than explain the absence of our erotic literature.

§

After thirty, I came to regard all time spent in the company of men a misuse of a precious and dwindling resource. My notion of decadence was to spend an evening *not* in the company of a woman. It turned out that I was, however, no decadent, and that was my ruin.

§

As his insults were no different from those I hurl at the mirror every morning, at least my enemy did not have the advantage of surprise. But then I understood: as is so often the case with such unguarded hysterias, he had merely provided a negative litany of his own long-unacknowledged virtues. Among these, it seems we were now required to account his beauty, his originality, his grace, even his fine head of hair. And at the thought of that aging popinjay gurning before *his* mirror each morning . . . I was suddenly mortified with pity.

It would be a great help to me personally if they would paint all the planes that are going to crash at some point in their service with a large black stripe. I abhor the way I am continually prodded into uninformed decisions.

§

I sometimes wonder if my meditations have won me anything more than estrangement, the right to wake up every morning as a bald white monkey with gravity issues.

§

My poor *Socialist Worker* friend . . . He confessed to me that he had just spent £180 on a new donkey jacket, which is now only available as an item of *couture* . . .

§

The emotional monotony of Neo-modernism. An anecdotal proof: look at how in *Amadeus* Peter Shaffer used Mozart's own music to illustrate every episode in the composer's life: his grief, joy, angst, love, his pranks, frustration, hilarity . . . Now: imagine a life of Schoenberg, similarly scored. In every scene – tennis court, birthday party, love-bed or deathbed – you'd be expecting an escaped lunatic in a fright mask to burst from the cupboard with an axe.

No one has ever adequately explained to me the self-evident merit in sensitivity. I spent my first seventeen years feeling everything, and the only place it got me was the mental ward. There is something base about art which provokes us merely to *suffer* more than we need to.

§

That night we saw through him, all of us, and he knew it. O it was a terrible thing to then watch a man try to *substantialise* himself.

§

It appeared clear from his letters and emails that this saintly individual was a petty and embittered monster. Then it later emerged, from the testimony of his close friends, that he was nothing of the sort, and capable of many discreet and time-consuming acts of charity. But then it further emerged, from the testimony of his bullied wife and damaged children, to what extent his friends were mistaken. And then one day they found his secret journal, where his own inner torment – as well as his early brutalisation at the hands of his father – was revealed, after which it was hard not to forgive him everything . . . Our error lay in our sentimental desire to read him as a recursive series, with each nested personality revealing a deeper truth. He was merely, like everyone else, a *mess*; an answer we are never satisfied with.

The brain is a tool for conjuring meaning from the void; and since the void is also our mother and father, it is a literal measure, if not of the void's *own* desire for meaning, then at least of its parental ambition.

§

What kills the writer, in the end, is the absence of a direct relationship between effort and accomplishment. Thus it is rarely true *work*, in any way our bodies can understand. A free day, all the kids off to their grandmother's, the house deathly quiet; half an hour's meditation; a cafetière of Java in the study; no sound but the rain dripping from the trees in the back garden through the open window . . . And I cannot introduce one word to another without them both falling out immediately. Today – exhausted, ill, overweight, the house full of yelling, my mind a roiling broth of fear and resentment and professional jealousy – a dozen problems I have pored over for weeks have been solved in twenty minutes flat. I end the day feeling worse than ever, as if I had accomplished nothing at all.

§

They awoke in a dark and windowless room, and all had forgotten how long they had slept. After a month of blindness they found a torch, which some declared an abomination, and retreated to the shadows forever. Then those with a torch found a watch, which read twelve; and some decided it was midnight, and some noon, and thereafter both parties developed their separate cultures.

Remove the error of self, and being here once is the identically equivalent miracle (if you can now conscionably use such a word) to being here again. The life now is already life after death, as remarkably so as any you might live in the future. Nothing will constitute the new you except the organism whose evolution has demanded, just as yours does now, the construction of another phantom centre. The next thing 'we' will indisputably know is another reawakening, the clever self-creation of the brief soul of something or other; though we might as well face up to the fact that—our infinite vegetable slumberings notwithstanding—we'll do well to make a rat or jellyfish; more likely some bizarre phenotype a few million light-years distant. The best we can pray for is that there is a secret economy at work, whereby a presently inscrutable, quantum-tunnelled aspect of our human schooling is converted to some universal currency and smuggled over. If I'm brutally honest, though, I can assemble little evidence to offer myself that I 'got lucky' this time round, and that the experience is worth repeating. What I think of as a fondness for being human is really just an attachment to being me – that is, to nothing at all.

§

No, I'm not obsessed with myself, just *the* self; I could be just as easily mesmerised by yours, if it were as readily available for study.

When her reputation was at its height a quarter-century ago, ah . . . ne'er had public opinion so well anticipated the judgement of posterity; she was *sui generis*, and dedicated her career to an elaborate proof of this fact, by elimination: not only was every writer wholly in the debt of some other, but her main aesthetic premise was that *all the things of the world* were in themselves mere realia, repro, helpless imitators of one another. Now her star had faded, she was obsessed with plagiarism, and saw it everywhere: it was the only way she could insist we were all still paying her homage.

§

Email allows me to indulge my new meditative technique: annihilation via impersonation. I answer each letter in my interlocutor's voice, and forty responses later I am no one and everyone.

§

The truer we sing, the more we violate our own boundaries, and the more our bodies protest; those who sing truest are all suicides.

§

My deeper ignorances I intend to cure by reincarnation. Not without its own inconveniences, to be sure, but fewer than the prospect of actual *study*.

The strongest illusions loom so close we are blind to them; they are continuous with our thought, and invisibly guide its content and direction. Original thinkers find the thumbnail purchase between the surface of their ideas and those distorting lenses, and then prise open the space in which they can look at them, not through them. Not without its dangers, as incompetence can mean self-operation on the *real* mind, which always leaves it damaged. (I think of my friend, now resigned to wearing glasses for life: waking drunk in the small hours, he was convinced he had forgotten to take out his contact lenses, and spent half an hour trying to remove his own corneas.) Alas, they so often emerge as the only means by which the dream can be brought into focus, and so must be sadly replaced in their original position.

§

I wake up crapulous and half-suicidal in a hotel room at 6.30 a.m., exhausted by my sweats and nightmares. I grope for the remote, and the breakfast show. A radiant woman is being interviewed, and the caption below her simply reads *Former Sufferer* . . .

§

The litany of my old lovers, my beautiful Linnaean taxonomy, my floral tribute.

I gave up origami in my teens because anything I created was closer to Neal Elias, the folder I liked least, than to a divine like Ligia Montoya or Yoshizawa. I have met many musicians with the same problem: one bassist spent his life practising to sound like Charles Mingus and ended up a double for the facile technomaniac Niels-Henning Ørsted Pedersen. But Mingus didn't practise to be Mingus; he sounded like Mingus after six months on the instrument. What made him Mingus was *not imitable*; it lay in a singular spirit, physiology and psychopathology. What *is* most imitable in a style, while perhaps the most superficially characteristic, usually emerges as the least enviable thing about it.

§

Only the best poets can risk simplicity. The rest of us are merely exposed by it. Only those same poets can risk complexity too: the rest invariably fail to realise the greatly increased responsibility towards *clarity* that it demands. Nonetheless so many rush towards it, knowing their faults are here best concealed.

§

The Greeks, right again. The light does indeed pour from our eyes – a dim, narrow human light: we stand before the world like a projectionist behind his dusty cone of shadows, illuminating only what we already know.

Certain events, if repeated often enough, allow their internal eidolon to be conjured at will. The fingertips on the fretboard, the slalom of the tongue on her thigh, the weight of the book, the screw on the southwesternmost quadrant of the cue ball . . . All these things access my realm of waking dream.

§

We were strolling along the street, and passed a couple of sleepy undergraduates. Suddenly my companion interjected – *so then I shot him in the face. Terrible fucking mess, brains all up the walls* . . . for no reason other than to bring a little colour into the lives of his eavesdroppers. He then resumed our conversation on Sondheim.

§

In this life, only *older* holds out the genuine possibility of our not being us.

§

The most disturbing thing about children learning to speak is discovering what homicidal whims have been preoccupying the two-year-old mind.

In our experience of the natural sublime, nothing is transcended except the human dream, as we are translated briefly into a state of simple animal belonging. Our revelation on these occasions is precisely *not* the Great Presence, but its summary disappearance – leaving us a happily earthbound monkey, suddenly and joyously continuous with their element. When God *really* dies – along with all his subtle and pervasive ghosts, his stubbornly loyal, reluctantly disbanding retinue – we're back home again. We have been utterly betrayed by those fancy intercessors of ours, who led us only into dismal exile.

§

When you respond by acting just as they do, low men immediately impute to you their own motives, and are torn between terror and camaraderie.

§

Lessons instantly learned: better to forget a woman's birthday altogether than to guess it six months out.

The laws of this particular universe favour creatures of a certain size, on planets of a certain gravity, orbiting stars of a certain optimum mass . . . And so on, for twenty other non-negotiable conditions. From which we can quickly extrapolate that the bicycle and the piano are almost certainly *universal solutions*. Nothing makes me more happy or more sad than the thought of my alien brother or sister sitting, right now, in a room so far distant not even light can pass between us, their rooms furnished with near-identical stuff . . . And dreaming, perhaps, the same cosmic solidarity – that dream, that thought, being the only thing we could ever exchange.

§

The reason for the pillow is that it eliminates the face.

§

Whenever he saw someone reading a Bible, he would spoil it for them by whispering, 'He dies in the end, you know.' I'm always tempted to do the same to anyone I see consulting their diary.

§

L. rather stagily 'insults my integrity', and expects me to be left reeling. I barely understood the offence. He was pulling a face at a blind man.

If I existed before this life and yet can recall nothing of it, then there is no 'I' that can be sensibly discussed beyond its present manifestation. Yet I have no doubt that I *have* existed before, simply because to say otherwise is to commit the Ptolemaic error of declaring one's present situation unique and miraculous. In this life my true family is a set with only one member; the minds of the others can be read but never penetrated. Nor can any fraternity be extended to the chain of my previous 'I's; all the links are uncoupled, and there is no lineage to pursue. Therefore my lives prior to this incarnation must encompass all the things that have ever been. Having no allegiance to any single mind, I discover myself nowhere and everywhere. My mind was there dispersed, and for fourteen billion years I partook of *all* lives, as the as-yet-uncondensed minds beyond my death now partake of my own. This leaves my present mind as a mere designated point, an inspissation of a universal mind that has condensed in me for no reason but the one it now chooses for itself: to uncover its own nature. I thought this a romantic fallacy, right up to the sudden and horrified registration of its demonstrable truth: we are matter; thinking is what we *do* here; therefore we are not the slaves but the primary agents of that universal mind. I have *sole responsibility*.

§

You've made a *blog* . . . Clever boy! Next: flushing.

§

Naturally, he had not once contemplated the possibility that the subject of his life's study might have been an idiot. His meticulous exegeses of the poems of X were about as edifying as the spectacle of a great scientist performing the microscopic dissection of a hamburger.

She insisted on absolute honesty, so I told her everything. I never saw her again, but at least I had spared the next guy the same ordeal.

§

Unthinkable that I would ever put my own happiness – whatever the hell *that* is – before anyone else's. Alas, when all the people whose happiness I had put first realised the extent of their company, they were considerably less moved by my selflessness.

§

The immaculate are tainted waiting to happen.

§

He could contrive, he knew, even an inauthentic suicide; his merely staying alive was his one concession to good taste.

§

I had never had such a thing before: a *declared* enemy. But I'd be lost without him now. It's a feeling so close to love. I *made* him, as one makes a poem or a child, by accident *and* design.

Critics all have this idea that authors inhabit another dimensional realm, right up to their first smack in the mouth – which feels to them quite miraculous, being their sex dream come true.

§

I was always pretty good at low-grade luck, those sad little two-cherry windfalls, and could always whistle up the yellow roof-light of the empty cab at three in the morning, the half-wish of the faint meteor, that wee treasurable frisson of the envelope icon on the mobile . . . But my psychic *aim* is catastrophic. There are days when I can make the phone ring at will, but it's always the last person I want to hear from. If you want some roses delivered out the blue from a secret admirer, I can probably arrange it for you, if you don't mind them being from your psychopathic driving instructor.

§

Faces rarely betray the true feelings of their owners, publicly or privately – with one exception: there is a tiny leakage in all acts of departure. If you attend, with preternatural care, to her eyes in the millisecond just prior to your turning your back to leave the room . . . There you will learn the very worst of what she thinks of you.

§

From the cloud to the zip-fastener, the silver birch to the dirty bomb, everything *arose* – and so must be considered a member of the set of natural objects.

The trouble with the blind eye is that it looks identical to the seeing kind; so either behave as if everyone can see you or *no one*, lest you be trapped in a lifetime of second-guessing.

§

Boredom, in its uncut state, is a *force*. To know it takes a mind of unassuageable restlessness – which pays that mind no compliment, as it implies neither curiosity nor any particular capacity for insight. Nor can such a mind ever disarm its own boredom by meditating upon nothing. Instead it perfects its obsession, its meditation upon *one* thing: in this we also lose the self, but bargain away the whole world too, in exchange for a profound intimacy with the Speyside malts, postage stamps, death, the feet of women.

§

When you first make love to the beloved, you enter a zone of unfocus as your face approaches hers . . . From which she reappears, in close-up, as a stranger. With anyone *but* the beloved, the experience is smoothly gradated; but such is the beloved's conflation with our *angel*, we know they have fallen to be with us, changed their essential nature for the sake of human love . . . And there our gratitude is bound to be mixed. Indeed, at first sight, she can look heartbreakingly close to the most terrifying thing you have ever seen.

§

Wouldn't it be wonderful if our children's religious education began and ended with the single sentence: 'Kids – I'm afraid no one has the first clue why we're here.'

He was no fool, and yet he had written a book by a fool.
As a dramatic monologue it would have been a triumph of
sustained impersonation, had we not suspected that *fool* was
the beginning and end of his literary repertoire.

§

Your manifest uncertainty is the best guarantor of the truth of
your statement, not your wise voice.

§

He liked to think of himself as a thorn in our side; but he was
a much smaller man than he imagined himself, and merely a
pain in the arse.

§

Doors, those merciful *conceits*, those blind eyes of the house . . .
As if your daughter or brother or friend wasn't beating off or
taking a shit six feet from where you stood.

§

By the age of eleven, I was finally exasperated with my parents.
I knew I had been left with no alternative but to fuck *myself* up.

A medium once told me that in my previous incarnation I had been a bluebottle who had caused an accident in a private plane, in which an evil man had been killed. As a result of that inadvertent heroism I had been karmically fast-tracked, despite the opposition of several high-ranking devas. I was immediately convinced of the truth of this story, and it continues to explain everything.

§

Allowed myself a smile this morning at a letter innocently referring to 'my love of the aphoristic form'. Christ – do you think if I really had a *choice*, I would write *this*? We occupy the margins through fate, not allegiance.

§

The fuel-injected articulacy of everything we write in a state of infatuation or anger. Latin for the fury; love's Anglo-Saxon tropes . . . No wonder poets wreck their lives trying to maintain these two states.

§

I have owed a slight acquaintance, K., an email for six months. This morning I hear that he has died. My single obsequy was to cross him off my to-do list, and feel my burden lighten a little. I even caught myself wondering if there might be something in this that could be worked up into a general strategy.

Of all the layers of dream that govern this life, the deepest and most catastrophic is that of our solitary being. Only death cures it, and even then only by cessation, not awakening.

§

We are all the thinking that matter does round here; but to acknowledge as much for one second would kill us outright. We are children, and not yet ready for that kind of responsibility. Hence our delegation of the whole business to our heavenly fathers and mothers.

§

'Now I'll read a *funny* poem.' 'Oh,' I thought. 'I'll be the judge of *that*.'

§

'Now I'll read a *long* poem.' It was then I finally admitted to myself that a poetry reading was no *night out*.

§

The self is a universal vanishing point.

'When I die,' he told me, 'I want every organ in my body to be completely *fucked*.' And so it was: they found his twenty-stone carcass on the sofa, soaked in spilt beer and melted Häagen-Dazs, smiling like the Buddha, and not a cell of him worth donating. As ambitions go, by no means the worst: to have exhausted the organism, to have wasted *nothing* . . .

§

I could not rouse myself from the nightmare; mercifully I was not alone in bed, and she heard my muffled cries and liberated me. The dream, I told her, was simply that I had no body to wake to, and hence no way out of the dream. Yet now that I was awake, it was no better. I knew I was still dreaming bodiless, and that not even death itself could spring me from it, and that all my life had been a mere diversion from this rising panic.

§

There *is* a universal eye, but it sees only through our own: our every blink blinds it.

§

I asked her what she thought had given our relationship its longevity, and so initiated – I quickly realised – the first discussion of our relationship we had ever had. We were finished in a month.

A day lost in failed spells, trying to conjure a ring from the phone: all those miserable countdowns to nothing, to zero, to no event.

§

Despite their not sharing a single physical or temperamental characteristic, Y became convinced he was the model for the protagonist in X's novel, and read the whole book as a litany of well-aimed, excoriating insult. His friends were worried for him, knew he was being paranoid and egotistical, and did their best to assure him of his error. X, meanwhile, shrugged and watched Y tear himself apart, knowing he had done his work beautifully.

§

Only someone with the *genuine* arrogance of a Rimbaud or a Cantona could declare their retirement and actually mean it. To make a single return to the stage is to reveal oneself a mere applause-monkey.

§

No, you confuse having entertained my idea with having merely *read* it; hence the ease of your dismissal.

I was so practised in disappointment, I absorbed the blow of her leaving me almost effortlessly. Allowing yourself to be *constructed* by the lover means you have been a different man from the start; I merely left his body behind like a husk, and let him take the punch. (I watched him double up, as from above.) The loveless wraith of me was then free to wander, looking for my new instructions.

§

I did not reciprocate her love until I realised the value other men had placed on her; and then who could *not*? Can any man honestly say that he accounts his worth in his own private and unique currency?

§

We always made love with our eyes closed; open, they were coupled by a fibre-optic cable, streaming intolerable terabytes of data.

§

The lapidary coldness of the aphorism assuages a grief or a grievance far better than the poem. It erects a stone over each individual hurt.

I think my unconscious plan was to involve her in an act of such intimacy as to both repel and enslave her: I had long understood the power of our disgusted complicities. But *nothing* could enslave her, *nothing* could repel her; and in reaching my own extremes I realised the game had been hers all along, and that I had lost my mind months ago.

§

Fate's book, but my italics.

§

Her so suddenly quitting in the early stages of our relationship meant I was obliged to hurriedly revise my future; at least this afforded me, I decided, the bravery of a blank canvas I might not otherwise have granted myself. Unfortunately, the new ventures and career paths I proposed – street vendor, lunatic, assassin, drunk – seemed oddly in the grip of certain imaginative constraints.

§

If you would win them back: know that the machinery of whatever game you were playing will execute a few extra turns from sheer momentum in the first few days of disconnected silence. Since most people insist on the game ending by its own rules and not its mere discontinuation, your mere refusal to play it (to do nothing, say, when that is *their* prerogative) will bewilder them utterly.

Imagining the worst is no talisman against it.

§

If only there was a poetic equivalent of that great sleeve-note instruction *play twice before listening* . . .

§

Our love poems are mostly the work of madmen. I laid them at her feet, proudly, as a cat would a half-eaten rat.

§

My friend is an egoist: every blank expression he reads as evidence of soullessness. I am an egotist: every blank expression I read as contempt.

§

He was obsessed with his fallibility, and I cared not a jot for mine. This, together with my gift for instant recantation, put me at a terrifically unfair advantage.

§

My time here has afforded me no enlightenment, though my night vision has improved enormously. In fact it seems to have evolved as if certain of its future indispensability.

With friends and strangers I can be no one; more and more
I confine myself to their company. Then one day I enter a
room full of *acquaintances*, and fly into a blind panic: I cannot
remember for the life of me who these people think I *am* . . .

§

He always whispered the bad news in your left ear, always
made sure his slanders were printed verso . . . For years he
escaped our attention. We knew, vaguely, that evil accompanied
him, but thought the two no more connected than the tree and
the wind that shook it. Then one day we realised there was no
wind: just his own black whistling.

§

Experiments in attachment. My friend has just paid for an
increase in his broadband capacity. I meet him in the cafe; he
looks terrible – his face puffy and pale, his eyes bloodshot . . .
He tells me he is now detained, night and day, in downloading
every album he ever owned, lost, desired, or was casually
intrigued by; he has now stopped even *listening* to them, and
spends his time sleeplessly monitoring a progress bar . . . He
says, 'it's like all my birthdays have come at once', by which I
can see he means, precisely, that he feels he is going to *die*.

I tried for a while to keep a diary, making one entry at dawn and another on the facing page before I fell asleep. (There are no meridian diaries; anyone able-bodied and under the age of seventy who has the leisure to write one is beneath contempt.) The irreconcilability of the two personalities was so immediately apparent, I quit after a few weeks. The dumb hope of one, then the disillusion of the other – a motif repeated without interruption – depressed me beyond words. I went back to bookending the days, as the human monkey should, with caffeine and alcohol, the newspaper and lovemaking, data and oblivion.

§

All evening, listening to his wonderful table talk, I kept finding myself think: 'Ah but in six months you'll be dead, and *I* will have said that . . .'

§

He prided himself on seeing through everyone. Then one evening, at a party, I saw how his focus always fell a little too far ahead of its object, and knew he had entered the realm of phantoms.

§

Silence between lovers always takes a negative or positive charge, and can't be empty or emptied of meaning; though if only one party understands this rule, they are in hell.

A fine recording by the seventy-year-old João Gilberto, still singing beautifully at an age when nearly every other singer has gone off . . . But there was nothing in his voice in the first place, no vibrato, no expression, nothing that could ever ripen and rot.

§

I enjoyed L.'s creeping senility. I could have him repeat my favourite stories as often as I wanted, sometimes several times in the space of the same afternoon. T.'s sudden lurch into his anecdotage, on the other hand, was a disaster: until then, his shyness had prevented our discovering what a bore he was.

§

Down at the clinic for my in-flight Valium, my usual doctor on holiday. 'How far are you flying?' asks the locum, reckoning the dose. 'Three miles up,' I reply, adding inwardly: *you idiot . . .*

§

In the end, the desolate age always turns instinctively to classicism, which if nothing else legislates against certain kinds of disappointment.

§

Language: the category error as belief system.

The rose's night-black is as true as her day-red.

§

It is possible for a woman to say, honestly, that she has thought of her lover all day long – but she will neglect to mention the twenty other things she has kept in her head at the same time. A man ignorant of this ability will be terrified by her declaration, since were it to be *his* – it would amount to a straightforward admission of his own derangement.

§

As we think of the dead, so the immortals think of us: as a fraternity of ghosts, the *ones who pass through* . . .

§

She was married, now – and happy, loquacious, twenty pounds heavier and the better for it, and given to fits of giggling. The metamorphosis had been so sudden, I had the clear sense that the woman in whom I had found such a black mystery had either been just another fantasy of mine, or stuck at some . . . neotenic impasse.

§

Nothing more dangerous than the saviour who mistimes his appearance.

Lying still inside her, I was suddenly freed from everything, my term, my fate, like a train that had run off the rails to find itself suddenly moored in the middle of a sunlit field, or a field in darkness.

§

The bleakest and briefest of human literatures, one I have seen men read and be straightaway moved to tears: the price tag.

§

When I lost my virginity, I flew my *own* sheets from the window, I *myself* bled with relief . . .

§

Eventually most musicians give up listening to their instrument, as I did, and hear only themselves; the real musicians never stop.

§

I still want to come back, one last time, as one of those beautiful charming men. But the line between their desire and the acquisition of its object is drawn so tight, they are vessels of pure karma; they can never depart the earth. To buy into such an individual once would be to buy into him forever.

The blush: what evolutionary advantage do we gain in the *publication* of our embarrassment? But then the secret shame rarely had much effect on my future conduct.

§

The singer has his guitar primarily for company, not accompaniment. As he ascended from the dark, it belatedly dawned on Orpheus that he didn't really *need* his girlfriend.

§

I'm always amused by those commentators who nervously insist that the working class's constant use of the word *fuck* is really just 'a form of punctuation'. It is, however, no more or less than what they dread: an inexhaustible river of smelted wrath, a Phlegethon of ancestral grievance . . .

§

The excluded first console themselves by deciding they must form a class of radical, then by perfecting a form of radical behaviour that guarantees that they will never risk the shame of being thrown out again.

I had been scrupulous in God's abolition; and nor would I allow the humanist error of allowing his ghost to watermark my thinking. But then I realised that I had the opportunity to resurrect him by simply *deciding* he existed – and, to my disgust, that there was nothing I desired as much. There was no sophistry in this at all; since the truth was no longer the possession of some inscrutable third party, it no longer existed to be determined, but unilaterally decided. I could construct whatever damn spirit I pleased. I mention this by way of explanation, should you one day find me torn to pieces behind the door of my locked study.

§

'But I don't *think* I could write poetry . . .' Unbelievably, my friend – a successful author in several genres – was serious; she thought there might still be the possibility she *could*, simply because she had never attempted it. Pointless to explain that she would have known from the age of five, or from her parents' stories of her terrifying fevers as a baby; that it is *something broken in the head* . . .

§

Dread and rapture are inimical to the composition of poetry, even if the naïf thinks them the ideal states. I'll never write a single decent word at 30,000 feet; if I try, I write black on black, or white on white. The temperament of the act and of the inspiration must somehow be oppositionally ranged, as the ink to the paper.

Beware the obsessive between obsessions: if his brain doesn't
eat itself, it will eat yours.

§

What have the poets lost now they no longer have their
mnemonics? The respect they used to arrogate to themselves
through the specific threat: *Would you like me to put something
in your head that you can't get out again?*

§

The worst thing about thinking nothing of yourself is that you
assume that your behaviour has no consequence. This makes
you much more dangerous than the egomaniac, who at least
spends all his time calculating for his own effect.

§

Blessed is the wrongdoer who makes no attempt to justify his
actions by anything but his *pure evil.*

§

Music softens us up for everything; the take-off, the poem, the
needle, the bolt.

What is it in the middle distance that implies our absence of attention? Short focus signs our concentration; long, our deep or distracted thought. But the eyes of the dead all converge on a point twenty yards away, presumably Death's own range.

§

It may indeed be the case that our new particle accelerators and supercolliders will allow MIT and CERN to verify the membrane basis of the universe in the next couple of years; this will conclusively prove the universe a monosubstantial unity. Though I have a terrible fear that they will conclusively *fail*. Ach, all those televised shamefaced apologies from the Dalai Lama . . .

§

'Trust me, you're *anything* but irresistible –' she said, 'you're just irresist*ing*.' At this she placed her hand on my heart . . . into which I felt it sink past the wrist. The self expunged in self-disgust is just as absent as any removed by more careful means, and folk can generally go just a little deeper with me than they can with most other people before encountering the resistance of another self. This slight fall they are wont to confuse with intimacy; it's merely the reflection I offer in lieu of a personality of my own.

My friend hated book jackets, and tore them all off immediately. I think he felt, somehow, that the book was still trying to sell him its contents after he had paid for them. Without its dust cover, the book is anonymous and valueless. You remove a book jacket just as you make a lover naked: before their complete possession, they must be removed from the *currency*.

§

There will always be one person who went to their grave knowing Shakespeare only as a moneylender, MacNeice as a poodle fancier, Feynman as a bongo player. The great and their little lives.

§

Many accounts of torture tend to confirm its vocational aspect; torturers will cheerfully put in a great deal of unpaid overtime. Another reason to accord 'the vocation' no particular respect; the word should be used with a deep neutrality.

§

I would hate that my Christian friend lose his faith. The dreams of the eternal agonies of his close acquaintances are his one source of real pleasure.

§

The lowest among the underclass often refuse name-contractions, which require the luxury of shedding a gram of identity. The children are all called Christopher, Anthony, Margaret, William, Alexandra.

Some women make nice distinctions that will ever remain a mystery to me. Today I asked a friend how her affair was progressing. 'It's not an *affair*,' she protested. 'We only do it in the afternoon.'

§

Sometimes it's hard to be a guy. We can surf easily between Chomsky's home page, Teen Anal, Theravada Buddhism and a cheat-code for *Grand Theft Auto* with scarcely a hiccup of bad conscience; the Net has externalised (and so part-socialised and normalised) a mental routine that hitherto had kept itself hidden, as we reasonably assumed such ugly, unmodulated key changes would be read as a sign of our moral degeneracy. Only an idiot would say this is a good thing, however; society is woven together by the collective denial of our nature. The leap from savannah to settlement to city was much harder for us, as our mind- and skill-sets were far less easily transferable. Had women not adapted so perfectly in a few million years, we would have cheerfully, and properly, taken another two billion over it.

§

Everything affirms the true faith. God's indifference is as much proof of his power as his intervention. The patent uselessness of prayer is joyfully understood as the corollary of his omnipotence – by which the believer understands his arrogation of *all* the power, their own tiny allotment included.

Yes I *know* Marcus Aurelius or Vauvenargues or Chesterton has already said this, and far more elegantly; but let's face it, you weren't listening then either.

§

Anthony Burgess, reviewing a new edition of the *OED*, tested it by looking up his favourite esoterica. He was pleased to find one particularly unusual word – but then saw that its single citation was given by Anthony Burgess. Did that supply a proof of the book's authority? Yes, if someone else looks up the word; no, if you are Anthony Burgess. Truth can be validated right up to its own front door, but no further, just as no god can confirm his own existence.

§

The speed of light is only the defining *conceit* of this place. Other universes will have fallen apart in their own fashion.

§

A stranger cycles past me in the street, then yells out at me, for no discernible reason – 'You useless bastard!' I felt like cheering him, as I would a magician who had just pulled my card from the pack.

§

I had badly miscalculated: when I kicked out God, he huffily took Satan with him, whereupon went my last excuse.

You are wrong about T.'s innocence being evidence of his 'good heart'; the fact that a washing machine or a toaster has no unconscious motive doesn't make it a saint.

§

I am sent a bundle of reviews and cuttings. I can now confirm that I have a small reputation as an intelligent and wise man; I also have another as an idiot and a fool. I have a small reputation as a man capable of courtesy and discretion; I have another as a graceless and loud-mouthed buffoon. I have a small reputation as a fine and original poet; I have another as an inept and derivative one. Accounting them all, they add up, precisely, to *nothing*.

§

First night of the flu last night. I dreamt, for what seemed like years, that I was a stand-up comedian, condemned forever to a disastrous routine of failed recognition humour: '. . . You know every time you count from one to ten, there's always one number over? You know when you go to the Gents, and there's always that smell of creosote in the first cubicle? You know how after you come and you're bleeding from your eyes and all these fucking *dwarves* show up?' It was no more than the amplification of my waking paranoia: that I have nothing to trade, that I am anecdotally bankrupt.

I wrote a blank poem once, which was immediately denounced as passé and unoriginal. But the basilisks that guard the original poems all hiss *cliché, cliché* . . . And sure enough, the gesture turned out to be not nearly as common as they had supposed. Indeed, a sad glance at my royalty statement tells me it is my most anthologised piece.

§

Went to see our new Hollywood Passion. Some kind of cultural watershed, surely: the point at which we finally succeeded in *exaggerating* Christ's agony.

§

The doors in the carpenter's house had been so beautifully hung they were impossible to open, having created a vacuum seal around their edges. He had to remove them all then replane their sides imperfectly, so his children could get to the bathroom again. This broke his heart. Our dreams so often surpass the world's ability to express them.

§

The beautiful can often only relax in the company of the ugly. This does not, alas, relax the ugly, but does lead to a great deal of bewildered sex between the two parties.

§

They awarded my Calvinist friend another prize, and he took to his bed immediately. He began to suspect a conspiracy.

After he had blessed my children, the Lama showed us to the door, still smiling hugely. Just before I pulled it to, I looked back and was shocked to see his expression changed utterly – bored, tired, cleaning his glasses. In my disappointment, I felt the sudden furnace-blast of my own ego. I'd once had a similar experience after an audience with a mortgage broker, and felt nothing but a satisfyingly rich contempt at his two-facedness; but the lesson was identical, and so too should have been my reaction.

§

Our human convention is that reputations can only properly be decided by posterity; though this has less to do with time than the mere addition of another couple of planets' worth of opinion, from which some common sense must inevitably prevail. But to be the size of Jupiter, and see those world-class charlatans, ass-lickers and nincompoops find their level *in their lifetime* . . .

§

So many of my moral crises turned out to be not my own but someone else's that I had been enthusiastically hosting. These proxy torments are more exhausting than any others, since one has to construct both the guilt *and* the sin.

§

I was always appalled when a former lover took a new one. I wanted a purdah of mourning, for the lot of them.

We have to send these books out *believing* they're good, and would not do so otherwise. The good review doesn't fill us with joy; it only returns us to a state of equanimity. The bad drives us to despair. Thus, at the end of it all, we can never be in credit. Publication is, let us never forget, a synonym for *exposure*, a straightforward exercise in shame.

§

An aphorism quoted in the paper – and the italics have fallen off yet again, presumably on the instructions of the same teenage sub who thinks that a semicolon is a full stop in a state of weedy indecision. For the last time: in a form with no context, overstressing is often a *necessity*.

§

God was only invented to protect the soul; the soul is just an erroneous back-formation from the ego; the ego is just an inwardly projected, spectral self-image which has arisen from the feedback loop of our individual consciousness, and that consciousness itself, only a tool possessed by a unit mammal which found itself in need of some half-decent predictive capability. In the name of which little skill we have immortalised ourselves, projected ourselves into an eternity on which we have not the slightest foothold.

§

My parents conceived me, the universe conceived of me.

I finally confessed to myself a vein of simple wickedness. This saved me a lot of time and energy I would otherwise have wasted in self-justification.

§

Of my male friends, maybe three have survived middle age with their hearing intact, and do not think almost continually and morbidly of themselves. (Well, maybe two; one died rather than face that possibility.) Nearly all the women have become less afraid. Even the childless know themselves to belong to a generative sex. But every man is a dead end, and he finds it out sooner or later.

§

The memory of the symphony, painting, film or novel is no more than that – a memory. But to remember a poem *is* the poem; hence our making a fetish of its memorability.

§

The holy book is a disease of degree. The first stage is the declaration of the text as incontrovertibly brilliant: this is the first step towards the elision of the author. As the book begins to slip the moorings of its lowly human origin, soon the text will be shown to have merely *obtained*, its vowelless words found on some tablet or monolith, itself merely a copy of some timeless and distant incunabulum. Note that the *Tao Te Ching* and the *Dhammapada* – two books that have become neither litanies of superstition, nor calls to war, nor lexicons of moral excuse – have both retained their authorship.

Foolishly, I buy a book on the strength of its cover quotes: several reviewers call it an 'instant classic'. It may well have been.

§

Heavens, it was a challenge, but I eventually found an insult he could not absorb. I suspect he was merely *full*.

§

People are their own blindspots. All well enough known, but the fact should be turned more often to our own advantage. For example: resubmit the work in the name of a rough anagram of the editor, and you will invariably find their opinion of it has dramatically improved.

§

A well-judged compliment briefly confers a cloak of invisibility on the one who pays it. While you receive one, hold on to your wallet.

§

After my ten-minute machine-gun raga guitar solo, my father threw me, gently, out of his country-and-western band. We are frogmarched from the genres by their guardians; they know that anything beyond the smallest mutations will destroy them. Postmodernism is really just a club for the turfed-out, for all those unwelcome Lamarckians, still bewildered at our failure to praise all the *leaps* they were making . . .

Try as he might, he could not get his face out of the mirror; to his great exasperation, he always blocked his own view. Of course deep down he knew that the transparencies he sought were not in the mirror at all, but to look anywhere else would by then have been inconceivable.

§

At enormous expense, he has turned the vast grounds of his country pile into a 'Garden of Cosmic Speculation', full of the most tasteless enormities: hills carved as double helices, hideous fractal patios, artificial lakes in the shape of strange attractors and equations sculpted in concrete. Some minor composers have been 'inspired', implausibly, to write works about it, and it is open to the public (here, the *priceless* detail) for just one day of the year. Behold, poor mortals, your Eden *today* . . . But the garden has long gone rotten in its knowledge, and come closing time we cast ourselves out again with inexpressible relief.

§

The ex-working classes can never quite believe themselves to be more than the sum of their good connections; too many of them assume that namedropping is one of the social graces.

§

He could never pay a compliment without bracing it on a slur; without it, he would have been flung backwards on his arse, as from a cannon recoil.

She was a burning bush, a screaming silence, and we were all incinerated as we leant in to decipher the white noise of her.

§

Terrifying, unthinkable – to realise that this universe only ever takes its form in the mind of one individual. No wonder we had to invent an all-seeing eye; the alternative was to place a near-infinite trust in one another. Without our gods to lift this responsibility, we would never have laid one stone on top of another, for fear all was phantasm.

§

Shocking to think that of all the million words I have typed into this machine it has not understood *one* of them. Yet I would not carelessly insult it.

§

The bare tree is still in the wind, as we are when we shed the leaves of our selfhood. Every thought slides through us like smoke through the branches.

§

M. is gaining a fine reputation for spotting great literary talent among the recently dead: they're barely cold before he's down at the mortuary, stitching the coat-tails to their blue arses. Having been stared over, through and past at one too many launch parties, he knows better than to ever praise the living again.

After a wretched, overlong and convoluted guitar solo, full
of badly executed quotes from Coltrane and Keith Jarrett, an
older musician whispered in my ear: 'Never be afraid of what's
easy on your instrument.' Indeed, what's easy is what is most
characteristic; what is difficult is what is against its native grain
and resonant possibility. Good general advice.

§

The last thing I have written is always my favourite because I
still host it; it is still me, is still in my body, in the wet red mill
of my brain, and your insulting it can physically injure me. Say
what you like about my first book, whose author is a complete
stranger.

§

Poets dream within their imaginative elsewheres. In Scotland
we live with very occasional illumination, so ours is actually a
rather sunlit verse; by contrast, the Spanish poet is stalked by
shadow.

Of the classes of metaphor, the prepositional is the most culturally insidious and hard to eradicate. There are underinterrogated consequences, for example, in thinking that we always write poems 'on' or 'about' a subject. In doing so we are often just extending our imaginative hegemony in another act of fatal misappropriation. We fall *in* love; so our lover feels entitled to assume that when our feelings undergo any complex change, we have simply fallen back out again. The Greeks thought of their future as behind them, and their past in front where they could see it; how much human misery has been caused by the dumb and hubristic inversion of that wholly sensible model?

§

Placing ourselves in complete chaos forces the creation of a centre. For those who have lost theirs, a good tactic of last resort.

§

Pedant at the guitar clinic: '. . . the available choice of *plectra* . . .' – both correct *and* a stupid affectation; the word is possibly current among concert mandolinists, but beyond that queer milieu you will impress no one but the shade of Fowler. Best speech lies in its judicious concession to bad speech.

I suspect the real 'trick' – if indeed it is a trick – with women is: (a) to simply love their company, and be unable to disguise it; and (b) to be confident enough either in yourself or your other arrangements *genuinely* not to care overmuch whether they will sleep with you or not. Feigned indifference is hopeless, and transparent. Desperation *stinks* to most women. But your visibly *not* hanging on the outcome of the evening is often a red rag to a bull.

§

Only the mad are safe from doubt. I am always bewildered by those who regard a revised opinion as a sign of weakness; it strikes me as a fine guarantee of the commentator's sanity.

§

It's monstrous to think of our parents having sex, because we then have to think of them conceiving *us* . . . Hard enough to live with the exile without replaying the scene of the eviction.

§

Glamour is a sister of Hope. As soon as the guns fall silent and we're fed and warm again, little Glamour creeps out from under the stairs, with her filtertips and kitten heels.

Good workmen blame their tools too; there's such a thing as bad tools. *Really* bad workmen utter no complaint, ask to be paid cash, and run.

§

A poem with one line wrong is like a Rubik's Cube with one square wrong: what it is precisely *not* is one move away from completion.

§

Never let the gesture drown the sign.

§

My best students have all regarded poetry as their secret shame, an exercise in disgrace.

§

One of the interesting things about mid-life, he told me, is that there is a very short period where your sexual partners might be drawn from a thirty-year age range. Then one night, purely aesthetic considerations do for one end, and justified self-consciousness the other – the light stays off, or the vest stays on – and the bandwidth shrinks by twenty years again.

Our 'wonderful variety of regional accents' has been achieved by ensuring that half the population can't afford to travel more than ten miles from their birthplace. Nothing guarantees cultural diversity like geographic isolation. (The St Kildans developed an incomprehensible form of Gaelic consisting mostly of speech impediments. Should we *rejoice* in this fact?) For the most part, this diversity can only be enjoyed by those moneyed travellers who can register the differences, which almost defines them as a class of cultural abstainer. As a *cause*, then, diversity can only be championed by those who least embody it. Not that any of this is wrong; just that we should accept that most arguments to preserve it are wholly paternalistic.

§

My fear of flying has absolutely nothing to do with a fear of death, but on the contrary one of being *alive*, in all its precarious horror.

§

God's joke, maybe, but he should work on his timing. I always had the feeling the Big Bang was a little precipitate. Nothing seemed *ready*.

§

I once sat through an hour of a man demonstrating his new technique for playing the saxophone: he sucked instead of blew. We punished him beautifully, however. We listened to him patiently; we gave him *every encouragement* . . .

The transcendental power of the dystopia. At the worst times in my life I have always sought to create them – socially, sexually, geographically – so that I might enact an *escape*, one which might then grow into a more generalised tactic.

§

All arts have their bass solo – the sestina, the lino-cut, the one-man play, those tours-de-force that we admire not because they survive their perverse form with any style or aplomb, but manage to do so at least without the total surrender of dignity; and that we applaud wildly, out of sheer *relief*...

§

R. has taken an *age* to die. We had reckoned on a few weeks, followed by five or six months' decent grace – then the brutal reappraisal of his work we all feel long overdue. Our frustration is starting to show, though. Any more procrastination, and we'll dismantle him where he lies.

§

Each white page, another invitation to the mark of genius! Suckered into ruining it every time.

§

Always plant a quiet line that critics can damn you with, one that will prove they were always hunting for it.

How often as a child I entered that infinite realm; yet I brought back not a single word to assuage my adulthood.

§

Sense is the carrier wave of truth. A tautology in all company but that of the Postmoderns, who it will one day strike with the force of revelation.

§

Writers can redeem a wasted day in two minutes; alas, this knowledge leads them to waste their days like no one else.

§

A brilliant idea at 2 a.m., so fine and original I had no need to write it down. Gone forever by dawn, of course. Proof again, if I needed it, that I carry the abyss inside me.

§

No matter how ill-matched they are, any couple stupid enough to have sex with their eyes open are vulnerable to love.

§

He was starting a little poetry magazine, and asked me if I had any advice for a budding editor. The only thing I could think of was *open all the mail away from your face.*

Just occasionally, this little nation of stoics makes me weep with pride. 'Happiness', he declared, his beer-glass drenching his shoes, 'is for *wimps*.'

§

Valium and Black Label; *enjoy the flight*; the declared prospect of heavy turb over Malaga, and three hours in which to anticipate it . . . Why, then, when I so often profess nothing but contempt for this heavy existence, this rage of the flesh? Precisely that: I have a fear of dying in the wrong element because it will not properly negotiate my release: *I cannot return my weight to the air.* I wish only to render to Caesar that which is Caesar's, and dread my life being derelict in its last transaction.

§

The bald ape has committed what is probably the universal *defining* error of the doomed intelligence: it has mistaken its dream for its element. Such carelessness will soon see it translated to the wrong one, where it will find itself irredeemably grounded, beached, drowned. If we're typical, no wonder the skies are silent.

§

Making a child is the opposite of killing someone. But there are still occasions when the former is the misdeed and the latter the kindness.

That exculpatory note, that letter that would come clean, explain everything . . . He spent so long drafting and redrafting it, he realised it would actually be an easier matter to maintain the lie and just outlive them all.

§

Such little memory as we recover from early childhood is really archaeology. In those seeds and potsherds we read the charmed domesticity of the ancient dead, moving through the day in their honeyed, eternal light.

§

The blessed lives we will not live: heaven is their promise, hell their abolition; but purgatory is their continual taunt, and its medium the living present.

§

My school-friend was incredulous: I had bought my father's old guitar with money from my Saturday job. Incomprehensible to the middle classes, of course, but the poor buy and sell from their parents and children, to seal their little money in.

§

In our self-loathing we are most beguiled by those who are beguiled by themselves; they are our only real ambition.

What kind of life would I have led without my glamorous double, who took all my missed opportunities? A tolerable one, for a start.

§

I am only too quick to credit strangers with either enormous sophistication or enormous stupidity; I flip between complete deference and complete condescension, so violently that I think of myself as two different men.

§

Astonishing, the number of mere acquaintances who immediately presume they have my confidence. If only they knew how hard my closest friends have had to work for it.

§

Personality is a mask we can't prise off, but no less a mask for that; only death removes it. When we feel it lift away from our suddenly weightless faces . . . we will experience our first real moment.

§

I love Auden's snarl at an underwhelmed boyfriend: 'If you want romance, fuck a journalist.' Yet the poet's proud lack of romance is precisely their romantic delusion – and, as so much of their art is predicated on it, they are prevented from giving it its real name: a pathological insensitivity to the feelings of others.

True zealots are betrayed by their admiration for their enemies, and their hatred of those who differ from them by one degree.

§

The poorest are denied their nostalgias by their social immobility. Their primal territories are the ones they still inhabit. Their sweetest memories are all ungeographic.

§

His corpse was beyond such trifling repose as mere peace. He had *left time*, and I could not help but reflect on the elegance of the move. Even my slow walk from the funeral parlour to the Tube station felt like an epileptic fit.

§

I stopped writing when my behaviour became so extreme as to cease to be representative. If no one but you can verify the accuracy of your insight – it is, technically, barren.

§

'So what did you think of my piece about J.'s book? I thought it was very *reasonable*.' (J. is an author I publish.) 'What review?' I replied, honestly. He was incredulous: '*What* review . . . !' No, I assured him I was quite ignorant of it. Then he gave the name of a small magazine I had barely heard of. It seemed otiose to remind him that the occasion for our conversation was J.'s own funeral, which he had obviously marked down in his calendar as another *soirée*.

When I move from noun to verb I disappear from the world.
To have only worked, slept, made love – and never once to have
noticed yourself, to die still *unacquainted* . . .

§

The soul is accessible only by sympathetic resonance, like the
horse's skull placed in the corner of the room by guitarists: the
mind can't touch it, but the true symbol, image or word can set
it moaning.

§

Between the ages of seven and twelve, I did nothing but study
origami . . . and for what? Four years ago, in a Belgian bar, I
folded Adolfo Cerceda's exquisite *Peacock* from a ten-euro bill
for a beautiful girl from Kiev. I recall Robert Harbin's marginal
comment on this model in *Secrets of Origami* – 'Now wait
for the oohs and aahs' – which, being all I have ever desired
from an audience, made the palms of my hands ache when I
first read it. Anyway, the girl reacted appropriately, I guess;
she widened her eyes, she made a little O of surprise; then she
flattened the note out and bought two beers. I *still* don't get it. I
can look forward to underwhelming my grandchildren on my
deathbed.

§

Possession by demons is only an inconvenience when they are
not fully assimilated.

I wouldn't sell my drafts for the earth. I wonder if I would ever have had a single decent review if they had known how I had cut these things from a block of raw error.

§

Speed up its evolution, and it becomes clear that the eye is not a receptive aperture but an exit wound, the catastrophic projectile fire of mind into the world.

§

All I learnt was discretion.

§

My new book arrived, and I had no idea who had written it. Or at least I now understood *why* I had written it: to expel the last man. Forgive the author of this book; but as you can see, I could live with him no longer.

§

An exhibition of Dutch art: Rubens has everything leaning this way, or that way, with all the dynamic nuance of a Thomas Hart Benton or Walt Disney. And then Vincent, who always understood that there are always at least three different winds in the sky, and that the hellish intricacy of their interaction is the reason we cannot hope to comprehend the motives or forces driving *anything*.

Those wholly estranged from themselves only have two real homes: the monastery or the stage.

§

On the clapped-out, bald-tyred council bus, hurtling down the dual carriageway at 70 mph in the lashing rain. All of us calm, reading, talking, absorbed, bored – but for one terrified dog, yowling and yelping as if he is being thrashed with a stick. The only sane animal among us, the only one still able to respond *proportionately.*

§

When poets are asked their occupation – that is to say what consumes their energies – they should answer, 'Not writing.'

§

Consciousness can no more unmask its own nature than the eye can see itself. It is contractually blind.

THE BOOK OF SHADOWS

Falling and flying are near-identical sensations, in all but one final detail. We should remember this when we see those men and women seemingly in love with their own decline.

§

Traditionally, the defining moment in a man's life arrives when he looks in his shaving glass and finds his father staring back; but there is a day so much more terrible we rarely speak of it – when he catches himself naked in a full-length mirror and sees his *mother* . . .

§

All that moves is ghost.

§

I run into a coeval for the first time in ten years. He has become monstrously fat. I tell him, truthfully, that it is a perfect delight to see him.

§

There were times, moving slowly inside her in the dark, when I would pause, and realise *I was not there.* Only the movement again restored some flicker of allegiance to the here-and-now from which we had all but been exempted.

We read according to an undeclared handicap system, to the specific *needs* of the author. We meet the novelists a little way, the poets at least halfway, the translated poets three-quarters of the way; the Postmoderns we pick up at the station in their wheelchairs.

§

This morning I was dreadfully constipated: mercifully, not a situation in which I often find myself – but *Jesus* . . . three-quarters of an hour, my forearms bracing the walls like Samson, attempting to gain one further degree of leverage . . . When the breakthrough finally came, suddenly and with some violence, I suffered the momentary conviction that I had expelled some vital gland or organ. God knows, the municipal statuary of a less prudish race would reflect something of the feats of raw heroism daily enacted in the narrow room. But now, my belt fastens easily, and I'm a little lighter, a little closer to heaven . . . Having made my votive offering to gravity, gravity relaxes its grip a little. Why did they never place this time among the canonical hours? Surely we're more air and fire now than ever.

§

A mercy, I suppose, that it ended. Any deeper intimacy with each other's anatomy would have involved a murder.

§

A perfectly *human* abyss: 'You felt so close just then . . .' 'I did?'

I was terrified when I suddenly realised her entire conversation took place in inverted commas. She didn't dare *mean* a thing.

§

Just as the tongue can no longer taste salt if all it tastes is salt; just as a certain stimulant will eventually clog up the synapses until it ceases to work on the brain – so the lover's body becomes slowly desensualised through its familiarity. Without its continual jittering saccade, the eye would be blind; it sees only by difference. When we cease to triangulate, the world disappears. As soon as we take another lover, and know another shape in our hands, another form lying below or above us – our partners, too, become desirable again. If we were creatures only of pure desire, this would solve everything.

§

When I was one or two I was obsessed with the lack of features on my parents' faces – the two eyes, the one lonely mouth: I would weep for them, for their blankness. I dread, now, to think of where I had just come from.

§

Writers often end up humourists if they read in public too often. Barring the odd and worthless snort of self-congratulation, laughter is the only *audible* response we can ever elicit. The silence of the unbearably moved and that of the terminally bored are indistinguishable.

The most efficient lies take only two forms: the truth in all but one detail, or a complete untruth. Anything between is amateurism: you are making the fatal mistake of enjoying yourself.

§

When I'm drunk, the ghosts of all my old lovers file through me one by one; I realise I had never stopped loving them, only buried them alive in me.

§

My work is the deferral of work, which exhausts me; the actual work I barely notice. As a result I never really feel like I'm working, a happy enough state of affairs for all but the Calvinists, for whom it is *an exact torment.*

§

Suddenly there was nothing I could do to impress her. All the brilliant discursion, the sublime compliments, the poems and songs I laid at her feet . . . I began to fear the worst: that if I was loved at all I was *loved for myself.*

§

Take-off again. That *inexcusable* hurry down the runway: frankly, nothing in life is this urgent.

The men and women who could change *everything* – Nature has sensibly cursed with sloth; they accomplish nothing but table talk and bitwork. The mediocrities found their cities everywhere.

§

We live in a human dream; being one in which everything appears purely in the guise of its human utility, and held in place by its human name. Names are small and sinister metaphors which restrict, absolutely, the use of an object. Our eyes open to this madness every morning; at night we dream within the dream; whole lives are spent without as much as a ripple of doubt on its surface. But when the object is allowed to shrug off its name, it begins the long road back to its own intrinsic mystery – and on finally reaching the core of its own estranging fire, radiates until the whole world is unified by it. The paper clip or the rose; either could open the path back to our awakening.

§

Already, deranged by love, he was thinking of revenge – even if he could not decide or locate the offence. Then it struck him: given her addiction to the vanishing trick, to her oblivions . . . he would *memorialise* her.

§

I no longer fantasise about being caught. I have long since apprehended myself; I am disappointed in me enough for everyone.

There is no day. The sun interrupts a continuous night. Our ancestors were correct: the sun abandons us.

§

All those chairs and bathtubs and cars and shoes which, emptied of us, are immediately returned to absurdity. How many lonely things we make for the world.

§

The speed of email allows us to develop sensitivities previously unknown to the epistolary arts. In the number of kisses appended to the foot of each message, we quickly learn to read not only the fluctuation of affection, but its disguise, its reigning in, and its cruel or flirtatious withdrawal. Connoisseurs of the *x,* after our affair was over, we tacitly settled on three: this exceeded the perfunctory, but didn't sign any inappropriate . . . revivals. Once, in a fit of enthusiasm, I added four. *I think you think I'm someone else* – the acid, instant response.

§

No matter how beautiful it is, if it appears in the wrong month: kill it.

§

Mediocre art is far worse than bad art. Bad art does not waste our time.

Every friendship demands loyalties that require the small betrayal of another. It is impossible to have more than ten real friends and be true to them all. Twenty and not a single one can trust you, nor should.

§

Terrible dream last night. I am standing at the window watching a great storm – the trees thrash around, the flowers flatten themselves to the earth, the grass dances wildly. Forgetting that you should never answer the telephone in a dream, I take a call, and learn that M. has died. I go outside and everything is still in complete frenzy, but there is not a single breath of wind.

§

When a great writer is discredited through revelations of their private life, we should reread the work immediately – it allows us the rare opportunity to assess it free from the seductions of *charm*. While this is the most volatile part of its appeal, we are still usually obliged to wait a generation after the author's death for it to evaporate.

§

Entire *years*, in total, thinking about sex. But then: entire years spent asleep. Heigh ho.

Almost everything in the room will survive you. To the room, you are *already* a ghost, a pathetic soft thing, coming and going.

§

Since it's only the idea that charms in conceptual art, the actual presence of the art itself affords no greater revelation. On the contrary, it reduces the imaginative possibilities of the concept to precisely one. Besides, conceptual art just sounds like a contrived synonym for *the book*.

§

Syntax confers power on its masters. The aspirant working class usually make the mistake of thinking it's *vocabulary* that accomplishes this, and are often – sinisterly – encouraged in this belief.

§

The Age, God help it. One occasionally takes its accurate pulse. This week, in love again, I turn *instinctively* to solace myself not in the *Song of Songs*, or in Burns or Sappho . . . but Roland Barthes.

§

In my adult life, the time I have actually lived inside the present moment would amount to no more than a single day. If only I could have *lived* it as a single day; it would have thrown its light into all the others, like a brazier in a dark arcade. Instead I find my way by sparks, and what they briefly make visible.

Even now, years later, I never make the mistake of sounding wholly well or content when I talk to her.

§

Good ideas prompted, bad ideas willed.

§

He was a man of such wide-ranging ignorance . . . it had real subtlety, depth, *reach* . . .

§

We were packing to leave the chalet; it was the first clear evening since we'd arrived. The sun was levelling like a carpenter's eye on the coast; and suddenly the effaced shape of every barrow and fort and souterrain stood up from the fields and hills in its black cloak, and the whole land, its whole human history, was readable again. I began to wonder if our own last night might not be the same, the shades of all our past lives standing up again, to be briefly reckoned and dismissed.

§

He is an almost worthless man; therefore we *know* our kindness to him a true charity. Worthless, but useful.

§

I would never claim to have her measure. However she gave me mine. My gratitude is . . . complex.

There are some of us most attracted where we know we'll
be most coldly dismissed, for whom the turned face – being
precisely where we came in, with *God forsaking us to the world
of men* – is actually our deepest possible nostalgia, and hell.

§

We lie down because the length of our shadows becomes
intolerable.

§

We learn from history and repeat it cheerfully. History does
not caution: it sanctions.

§

Yes, there are only *ever* misreadings, of course. But mine is the
correct one . . .

§

Only the insecure age valorises the individual voice; not least
because it encourages the radical artist towards a form of
speech far easier to identify and suppress.

The worst atrocities are derelictions not of the spirit but of the imagination. Babi Yar and Nanking were supreme failures of the human imagination. If you can imagine how a tortured child feels, your identification is instantaneous; you banish the thought before it even arises. Naively, I used to think that this reflex was fractured only in the psychotic.

§

He lost so much in translation I now suspect him of having *gained.*

§

I was cavalier with her secret. It was never *my* secret; I envied her for it.

§

Poetry is as much a mode of reading as of writing. We can read a poem into anything.

§

Some people achieve their humility by prayer and fasting, some by great charitable works. My own method is to behave in public like a complete moron every three months or so.

There are writers for whom no forms exist: too clever for novels, too sceptical for poetry, too verbose for the aphorism, all that is left to them is the essay – the least appropriate medium for the *foiled*. They all end up critics.

§

Don't mistake petrifaction for inner strength. The walking dead often appear impossibly stoical to us: they are.

§

We turn from the light to see.

§

Speech is just a very complicated form of song.

§

No fury more righteous than that of a sinner accused of the wrong sin.

§

In some Neanderthal part of me, every husband poses an affront.

Appalling that so many of my imagined triumphs still take place before my second-year school assembly, who will finally vindicate me . . .

§

Only the rarest artists move towards simplicity. The rest *progress*, which invariably means complication, as if you measured your advance by the number of readers you leave behind.

§

Reading how Edinburgh died in 1750: *Apoplexy, Ague, the Rising of the Lights* . . . Even death has its fashions. The biotechs, dying of their short-outs and faulty algorithms, will look at our cancers and thromboses as quaint forms of *hysteri.* . . .

§

Each time I revealed to someone my last undeclared deceit, I was compelled to perpetrate another. If something of me was always concealed from everyone, I would always know some small part of ghosthood.

How often I've mistakenly returned to an early draft, and made the same tiny changes I had already made a month earlier. Though I take this less as a token of the work's smooth march to its imago than an identical state of shortfall; others would have done better. Everything might start by heading straight towards my dream of it, but is slowed and then halted at the limit of my contract, my karma, my luck.

§

There was no point in dedicating myself to besting the rival suitors. Unlike them – *superior* to them – I knew her real worth; I spent the time looking over my shoulder for Odysseus.

§

Wise never to sing the glories of the age too loudly; this is why we are stuck with constellations called the Air Pump and the Microscope. Either that, or we reconfigure the heavens every fifty years – perhaps it would be chastening, in our old age, to stand in the frosty night delineating for our grandchildren the glorious outlines of the Mouse Mat, the Fax Machine, the Cyberpet.

§

Our translator friend suggested, in all seriousness, that there should be a new Nobel Prize – for translation. My first response was to agree, but also propose Nobels for dentistry and cheese-making; though I should have been harder on him. Especially as nearly all non-poet translators of poetry fail to understand the poem's incarnation in its tongue is *all there is of it*. They look at the Mona Lisa, then make a picture of a woman smiling.

Terrible description in the newspaper today of a woman watching her child fall, fatally, from a high playground slide. 'It was as if everything went into slow motion . . .' But time had not slowed; she had hesitated, our human instinct being to watch first and act second. Can you imagine a lioness in such a paralysis of *spectatorship*?

§

The priestly good looks, the almost ostentatiously plain wife . . . His saintly expression a reproach of sorts, insofar as you had to suspend dealings in your usual currency – you wouldn't dare tell the mildest story against a *soul,* knowing he'd never take your side. There was a time when I used to think that such a man brought out the best in people. But since he rejects *all* allegiances, which are only forged against something or other, we all leave his company perfectly disgusted with ourselves.

§

Roll on the biotech phase, please; if only to stop all this *sweating* . . .

§

What my cabal look for: quick eyes. (The quick brain is another matter.) When we see those we immediately acknowledge a brother or sister under the curse of the present moment.

Disconsolately toying with my £20 plate of saffron risotto
in some ramshackle private club in the company of a comic
librettist, an agent, and a publisher of erotic literature –
the C-list to which I obviously aspired – I knew as much
abasement as I would have found in Gurdjieff's commune,
in the driving rain, standing in the bottom of a hole I had
been digging for a week, a hole I had been forced to dig *for no
reason*. The lessons we need we find anywhere.

§

Seventy years. But your childhood was an infinity. What fools
we were to sign up to time.

§

If I knew that, like Picasso, I might remain sexual *to the end*
– I'd probably make no attempt at reform. So much male
'selfwork' is just the dignified accommodation of one's own
decrepitude.

§

If I try to write anything longer than a single sentence, I find
myself just making things up.

Though we acquire an air of inviolate religiosity in our solitude, nothing makes us less human than a solitude interrupted; specifically, the monophone treble obscenity of the *William Tell* Overture on the mobile phone of the guy opposite me on the train, his huge red spectacles, his yelled bonhomie . . . I find myself praying that his next call will bring him news of the death of his mother.

§

In bed she had the trick of indicating everything with complete explicitness, while still managing to communicate entirely by way of euphemism and babytalk . . . Like the 1,000 names of God, as if the world would vanish if she were to articulate the *cunt*. Suddenly I understood the mystery of the palladium.

§

Women are better than men.

§

In all literary matters, to delete in error is better than to include in error.

§

Well, critic: fair criticism. But at the end of the day, she did; you didn't – and you still think this is a *trivial* distinction?

Anal sex used to have one serious advantage: there were few cinematic precedents that instructed either party how they should *look*.

§

Translated verse is usually given away by the strenuous informality of its delivery. As if you had presented your passport and visa before anyone had asked for it: such behaviour only arouses suspicion.

§

We were fools or mutes or children around each other. The conversations had all taken place lifetimes ago. Our love *began* in redundancy.

§

Zero-valent: of an atom that cannot combine with any other. Though the attribute alone turns its subject to an atom. Those weeks when she felt herself undergo a kind of centripetal collapse, spinning to almost nothing, like a star in its last days, a nothing with a terrible weight at its exact and more exact centre.

§

As soon as we become reconciled to the fact of the road and to no end of any kind . . . then we know something like serenity.

I cannot read more than a line of anything Hartley Coleridge or John Clare wrote, even a scrap of correspondence, without being reminded of what Rilke felt towards dogs: he loved them so much he could not bear to be in the same room as them, so appalled was he by 'these creatures . . . we have helped up to a soul for which there is no heaven', and their curse of feeling *everything*. John Clare, John Clare, even his name flays me.

§

The Scottish Buddha, drunk under his whin-bush, preaching the annihilation of the self through *disgust alone* . . .

§

Any series of brilliancies, like those million exposures we suffer cycling down a sunlit avenue, begins by exhilarating us and ends in nausea and disorientation . . . As mature readers, the fireworks might still dazzle, but the longueurs sustain us.

§

Too late for everything; not too late for anything; I flip between death and eternity, and either way nothing gets done.

§

After a long period of reflection, he decided that he was in fact right yet again.

She had asked that I mark her, more than once. That exact half-millimetre-give of her flesh in my teeth as it took their imprint, the sweetness as I lifted the blood through her skin . . . I could hardly raise as much as a pale blush. It took too *much* to mark her.

§

Whenever we return with music from our dreams, it retains its beauty; the beautiful line of verse, though, oxidises on its exposure to daylight, and turns to gibberish before our eyes. No better proof that music pays its line far more deeply into the unconscious. Poetry is the music of consciousness.

§

I spoke to a man whose meditational practice, for one entire month, consisted of visualising his loved ones as skeletons and putrefying corpses. It did indeed allow him to live within the present moment all the more authentically, at the very flickering cursor of its transience. But one year on he could still not make love to his wife, for the horror.

§

Consolations of egomania. How often in his life did he mutter to himself, *grit your teeth and think of your biographers . . .*

The untarnishable brilliance of lost work . . . I remember a sequence of comic stories I completed when I was ten years old, and thought very highly of; then my horror when, a year later, I realised I'd mislaid them. Even now, I still have the feeling they would have secured my reputation.

§

At least I could explain my jealousy in Darwinian terms: it allowed me to *overprize* her.

§

When I turn away from a man and woman she grows wings and he grows horns. I counter the feeling by speaking well of him immediately: *Yeah – nice guy, nice guy, nice guy* . . . my spell against demons. Against the wings I have no protection.

§

It now transpires from an analysis of Einstein's brain that, as we suspected, he was less an exemplary specimen than a freak; *upon the shoulders of mutants* . . . Any other species would have smelled him a mile away, and torn him limb from limb at birth, or left him out for the jackals and vultures – every other animal possessing a perfectly sensible terror of innovation. Only a doomed race could prize it.

Amazing the insouciance we learn to affect in the face of the worst thing. Every evening, part of me still wants to rush into the street screaming 'Jesus, can't you people *see*? It's getting *dark* . . .'

§

If you were offered one hour or two, would you really choose two? Now: work backwards.

§

W. miscalculated. He thought he was overexposed and would be valued for his rare appearances. Within a year they had forgotten him.

§

We're forever reading atrocities as mere omens; anything to do nothing a little while longer.

§

It's not our love we demand to have reciprocated, but our need. We can habituate ourselves to the imbalances of the first; historical and literary precedent have even provided for them a certain nobility and tragic lighting. Unrequited *need*, however, turns the sufferer monstrous, pathetic, exposed, a naked giant in a diaper.

To renounce not *the* self, but *your* self; somehow a very different proposition.

§

Rejection quickly breeds an unnatural viciousness of style. Nothing is so conducive to a lyric and contemplative art as early publication.

§

If only art were a matter of luck, of very occasional discovery, like those absurd rubies and emeralds and gold-seams that turn up from time to time in the Outer Hebrides. Then we could dispense with the *artist* . . .

§

I am berated by a young gunslinger of a drama critic for my 'naive and passé symbolism'. In my next play, a young gunslinger of a drama critic is yanked from the audience, hung and disembowelled in the first scene. I take a deep satisfaction in the thought that even he – however naive and passé he may feel it to be – will find in this no trace of the symbolic whatsoever.

After the events that befell T. – his tragedy was inconceivable, *exceptional* – my immaculate friend did not know how to behave when the subject arose. The situation was absent from her book of protocols. Instead she adopted a robotic neutrality, from which vantage she could observe our shamed and inarticulate flailings. In that moment I saw through her completely.

§

Why is it I mark the passage of time in my friends' faces with such horror, and in my own with such equanimity? And why do so many women I know suffer the inverse curse?

§

My project of memorising all the wild flowers of Scotland is going remarkably well; last week, a rare kind of butterwort, a pyramid orchid, an eight-petalled wintergreen . . . all part of the grand plan. Soon I'll be as dead to them as I am already to the poem and the song, I shall have increased my *immunity*. At times like this, I begin to understand the passions of the early anatomists.

§

A stark choice that night: do as she wanted, turn up at her place, fuck, and inevitably contract the vicious flu she's carrying, or make my excuses and stay home. Inevitably, the former. I loved her; besides, I found it intoxicating to think that I was infecting myself so . . . voluntarily, and denying the virus its usual satisfaction in seeking me out.

All my teachers have been women. Although several men have taken me aside for an hour to tell me things they know.

§

I read a definition of the word *solid*: 'something which retains its shape'; and find myself immediately terrified by the *wilfulness* of objects.

§

The grim secrets only a practitioner can tell you: for example, if only you knew how infrequently musicians actually *mean* it . . .

§

B. thinks and talks on his feet more brilliantly than anyone I know. I'm always consoled by the reflection that this facility has had the effect of eroding, to the point of extinction, any allegiance he had ever felt to the truth.

§

Our dreams can also be mediocre. Yesterday I read an obituary of F., 'a true visionary'; maybe, but his visions were second-rate.

§

In all art, the function of the ego is to drive you to the gig, then keep the van ticking over while you perform without it. Those who fail to do so are easy to identify: they all *shake*.

The only pure suicide is self-strangulation; everything else requires the world as an accomplice. Best was Yogananda's *mahasamadhi* – announcing his departure at the dinner table, and raising his third eye to the crown chakra; such acts implicate nothing else in the universe and are surely committed with no karmic consequence. Perhaps that is the *only* act.

§

Our American genius is in town . . . No one can recall the title of a single poem he has written, yet his eminence goes unquestioned; were he to write one really memorable line, his reputation would collapse. Nothing disturbs the perfectly unreflective surface of his composure, not the lowest brilliancy.

§

The drawn curtains in the morning, brightening and darkening like some savage commentary on the fickleness of the human mood.

§

Amazing that the chess clock never found a more general application. A more enlightened society would have made it as indispensable to conversation as shoes to walking.

Strange ceremonies no one told you you would have to observe: the first lover to die on you. You've made love to a dead woman; the white limbs that were folded round you only last year are already rotting into the earth. You *must* have missed something the last time – some sign, some undertone of *départ* to the proceedings.

§

I was delighted to read in a biography of Adolfo Cerceda, the great Argentinian magician, that 'he survived surgery for a malignant tumour on the lungs, and on his recovery embarked on a world tour, this time changing his name to Carlos Corda'. I immediately saw that there were two or three occasions in my life when a better instinct would have compelled me to act in the same way.

§

Gravity fluctuates.

§

A few superstructural facial muscles, that business with the thumbs, a certain delicacy over the matter of cannibalism . . . Otherwise no difference worth the name.

§

Like a fool, I let her know she was on my mind *all the time*. Specifically I was telling her that I *haunted* her; then wondered why the news appalled her so.

[157]

Time + consciousness = foreknowledge of our passing. Our only *unique* gift; we can act knowing, in some sense, that we are already dead.

§

I'm *terrified* of my euphorias. Influenza or despair is a day away.

§

The trees in winter, those exact diagrams of all our dead yearnings.

§

For all his virtues, what a master of overstatement he was; he never understood that a portent needs its mundane context. He would fill the sky with comets. But against the mediocrity of his English contemporaries, he was *himself* an omen, which is why the time required him. Too much, perhaps, to say that he lent his poems much of their poetry; but we also miss *him*.

§

The night we first met, I remember standing at the bar, and being almost floored by the most astonishing and unannounced pain in the head . . . I almost passed out. Some part of the spirit clearly knows the track; I'd come to some fatal junction and taken a brutal jolt as I crossed the points.

A poet has four lives. First, that of their lyric innocence, when they believe the word and its object to be perfectly interchangeable. Next, the one they lead after waking up to the fact that a poet is someone whom words continually *fail*; the word, in fact, falls terribly short of the world, and – the quieter but larger revelation – this very inadequacy has been responsible for the preservation of their sanity in the meantime. (Only the mad have true equivalences, and will greet you as their mother, or tell you that the cellar door is the gateway to hell; the poet only indulges the possibility.) Now he must pass through that dead-zone most poets enter in midlife. By now thoroughly suspicious of the entire enterprise, he leaves the tiny house of the poem to inspect the facade, and learn something of the architectural mysteries he once had no desire to penetrate, such was his dumb faith in their ability to shelter him. And there he stands in the neat little garden, admiring the proportions of the walls, the deep, unearthly indigo of the shutters, the strange hexagonal tessellations on the roof. *It looks like a tiny fane to a banished god*, he thinks to himself, fatally, as the door shuts in his face. Then he spends his years in the alyric wilderness; till one day, returning to the house more through sorry nostalgia than hope, he finds that the back door has been left off the latch all along. So, with qualified rejoicing, he enters the fourth stage, and regains his lyric muse – but never forgets that this innocence must be conscientiously, even cynically defended (something you can hear in the willed artlessness of certain older poets). In his little temple, the word is the world again, and he is safe from both madness and disinspiration, provided he looks through the windows occasionally; an activity to which he must daily urge himself and – as crucially – restrict himself entirely.

Time heals so well it erases us; we *are* its wounds.

§

The present tense in English is too sibilant to be of much use to poets.

§

All our trouble starts with Adam, and his onomastic fetish. Since then everything has been in pieces.

§

That night I ground on, replaying in my mind the first scenes of our lovemaking. It was for that earlier woman I cried out; or for that time when, in the infinite tenderness of our regard, we seemed almost to create one another, to lift each other up into the light . . . before our looking turned into mere exposure: that cycle of quotidian betrayal, that hunger that leaches all the mystery from a face, like the colour and perfume from a bottle of scent left too long in the sun.

§

We love all random arrangements; they seem to invite us to *divine.*

If we *really* believed a word we said, then – like Socrates, Jesus, Buddha – we would just think aloud. But as small artists, we're morbidly concerned with the dissemination and preservation of the text – from bribing our reviewers and securing our book-club deals, right down to fretting over the stitching and the acidity of the paper. The real prophets always know their words will be carried for them, and are carved into the tablets as they hit the air.

§

Less is pretty much the same.

§

Remember that the Fibonacci sequence starts with the repetition of the One. Our lives converge on their golden section by the same initial tactic: the duplication of the entire universe in our infant minds.

§

Jealousy destroys every aspect of the lover's performance. He can no longer make a good joke, write a decent letter, and least of all fuck – being instead drawn into one black, inwardly blooming thought that seems centred not in his brain but the solar plexus. Here he enters into that infatuatory contemplation of the rival, while his lover becomes only a cipher for her own betrayal. I deny any homoerotic subcurrent here, however. I had no way of describing my feelings towards him – whose only crime was to *see her breast* – until I read of Cuchullain's warp-spasm in the *Tain*.

No email for an hour. The *bastards.*

§

Only the incremental advance is consolidated.

§

Though it seems impossible to believe that My Lai was *ever* (I read here) a 'sleepy village' in South Vietnam, or Thalidomide an anti-emetic, so it must have been. No name is guaranteed its innocence forever. Right now, in your immediate line of sight, there will be one thing – a postcard, a foodstuff, a brand-name – whose apparent inviolate banality will become a horror within your lifetime.

§

I've noticed that whenever I feel compelled, *for no good reason,* to look at my watch, it's almost always ten to three. Why on earth should I lose track of the day at this point, as if time itself had slipped a cog? We all know the imp of accidie, who strikes as the sun reaches its zenith; but there are others – *personal* demons – who sit upon certain angles of the clock-hands, as patiently as a vulture on a rock. God knows what *they* are preparing for us.

Consistency – whether of argument, opinion, or 'voice' – is only a virtue in the individual opus. Only sentimentalists and the terminally insecure demand that oeuvres or *lives* should aspire to it.

§

All true poems are fugitive, being embarrassed by their human source.

§

So much time is wasted mistaking the indifference of our acquaintances for deliberate slight. We would be in everyone's minds all the time, as we are in our own.

§

Inconveniently, books are all the pages in them, not just the ones you choose to read.

§

I came home. I had grown sick of my accent.

My admiration for him was too high, and destroyed any chance we might have had of friendship. Every email to him I drafted and redrafted into idiocy, solecism and quixotic affectation. I began to resent him, to devise ways I might discredit him, *depose* him . . . and then to understand why he had been wary of me from the start.

§

Like every other literary critic, Bloom credits the writer with far too much interest in literature. Such as it exists, the anxiety of influence is mostly a business between contemporaries. The tensions are all sibling, not Oedipal.

§

Difficult to understand how such kindness and such a pure vanity could coexist in the one man; clearly, it's more than just the Sisyphean project of clearing his conscience. It would almost be enough to restore my faith, if I only knew in *what*.

§

He has made a career of his immaculate surface. To hear him order a drink or receive a compliment is to witness a marvel of tact and eloquence; but now everything in the world disappoints him. Though he has become so vitrified, so *deeply* surface – he will not crack, but shatter.

Discovering it in a friend's novel, R. frets and frets over the phrase 'her beautiful and unfashionable body'. A cruel thing to construct such a perfect compliment, one he knew would torment her, and only her.

§

'Not *can't*: *won't*.' The remark, though only a mother-in-law's snarl over her vegetarianism, obsessed her. Her secret refuge was that she had no choice to make in anything – less a fatalism, however, than a kind of ossification of the will. She might, she thought, be wholly imperfect; but at least this steady state removed the exhausting and pointless movement towards an impossible perfection.

§

The sex was utterly straightforward, being, for once, a direct means to an end. I know we were annihilated in love. Couples should not say *we were one,* when they mean *we were nothing.*

§

Always an error to make someone profess what they will not volunteer – especially in love, where the spontaneity of its declaration is all the language ever holds of it.

§

Such is E.'s need to be loved, he experiences the casual indifference of a stranger and a snub from his closest friend as the *same torment.*

The lyric efflorescences of youth and old age are only partly mysterious: they are the only two occasions where one can work outside the shadow of criticism. The young poet cannot anticipate it, and the old poet need not.

§

Our empathies have to be set to the correct aperture. An hour ago, I interrupted my writing to take coffee in the front room; the arm of an old chair had come loose, and appeared to be raised in a gesture of helplessness . . . I was overcome with a ridiculous sensation of pity, and almost had to check myself from dashing over and helping the thing to its feet. Then the aching, lidless stare of the window, the huge weariness of the walls under their weight of books, the carpet's torture of knots, the hundreds of pounds of tension driven into every string in the wretched piano . . . It seemed to me that we'd filled every natural thing with our own torment.

§

I have taken pleasure in thinking of the worst things, over and over and over, for so many years now; amazing that they still produce any frisson. I suppose this is how we establish the *incorruptible* taboos.

§

X's honest and atrocious vice is that she values only what is valued for her. She is so attuned to the tiny hourly fluctuations in your celebrity, you can read them off her like an altimeter. There are days when she would throw herself at your feet, others when you could not get her attention if you fell down dead at hers.

The realm of the infinite states, those ineffable, discrete, impossibly various moods of my childhood, I neglected to cultivate simply *because* I could not apprehend them in language. I wander in, occasionally, through the usual open doors – the edge of consciousness, the sense of smell . . . otherwise: utter neglect. The spell of music can sometimes raise them. But if I could make just *one* reproducible – even the bleakest and most melancholy – its quality of the eternal would make for a far richer life than the one I endure.

§

We feel nothing only under general anaesthetic. I've heard it said that the mere existence of those superb lacunae negates the possibility of an afterlife. I disagree – though they probably show that there is nothing in the next life that will have any currency in *this*. Who knows what angelic conversations we were forced to hand over at customs, before our climb down into the recovery room?

§

Only having children makes any sense of our *biological* contract. Finally, some reward for the torment of those drip-fed poisons, reptilian tics and Neanderthal lunges whose derangement shapes half the day.

§

The capacity for suffering is relative to the suffering; for some, a slight discomfort is as intolerable as passing a kidney stone. Hence the writers' sincere belief that their cramps and boredom qualify them to animate the worst things that have ever happened to us.

Any vice or virtue, sufficiently cultivated, will eventually simplify a character into subhumanity. The saints are as incomprehensible to us as the monsters.

§

I try to write rejections of meticulous kindness. Some are sent sincerely, others insincerely, and only I know which. No: *all* are sent sincerely . . . the bad poets are mollified, the talented encouraged, and everyone's happy. It seems unnecessarily cruel that those snubbed by the muse on an hourly basis should have to endure a further rebuff from an opinionated nonentity having a bad morning. Hell, some of my *best friends* are talentless.

§

X sits in the middle of a field, in the invulnerable heart of what he thinks of as *the right,* less nursing his grievances than breeding and crossbreeding them – before sending these razor-toothed and taloned monstrosities out into the world. But we would not feed them, and now they are ravenous, and homesick.

§

Not as clever as he thinks he is – the one criticism I could always inwardly dismiss and which never touched me. My low opinion of myself is *inalienably* mine, and thus supremely qualified – and to that extent, irrefutable.

Versatility is the most double-edged of the artistic virtues, since it allows every critic the latitude to find something a little closer to themselves or their demons than they might otherwise have discovered.

§

The sadness of old shoes. Putting them on again, I suddenly remember all the old friends I haven't seen for ages; and then *why*.

§

A correction made to work more than five years old is less a revision then the cancellation of the opinion of another man.

§

I realised why I could never have married her: when she fell asleep, she put on a coat of lead. No man ever felt so alone as one who spent a whole night with B.

§

In any other religion one would be shaken by a master's failure – so what is it about the falls from grace of Chögyam Trungpa and Sogyal Rinpoche that seem to *validate* their teaching? Just as the destruction of the Bamiyan Buddhas was a glorious lesson in transience; a reminder that there is no one worth following, only paths.

A style is a strategy of evasion.

§

Our human advances are less so than a continually exploding view of our minds – our cars, televisions, saxophones, tea towels and bombs only long-inchoate motifs that found their timely incarnation. However surreal and complex the outer edge of their proliferation starts to look, we have to remember it was all contained within us, always, somewhere in the fractal detail of the blueprint.

§

Only the dead have a past. As long as we breathe we can be called to account for everything.

§

By examining the range of his sexual experiences, a man can judge the depths to which he can sink and the heights to which he can ascend in this lifetime; but he must remember it's only the scale, never the *means*.

§

At last he found his real silent muse. Until now, he had made do with the imaginary, the dead and the indifferent (and once, shamefully, a clinical deaf-mute); but how could he have known that her silence would be such an abomination? For the first time, it was the sound of the word *withheld*. And *what* word . . . he would waste hours in petrified speculation.

I began to relish – to venerate and luxuriate in – that long
five-second amnesia as I came to; that gap where, though
conscious, we have not yet remembered our bereavement or
terror or mad love; where we perceive that our enrolment in
the world of pain is in fact entirely voluntary.

§

X produces a marvellous elegy. The hapless Y, mad with envy,
writes one where otherwise he would not have bothered. The
result is a triumph of self-aggrandisement; he dishonours
himself and his dead.

§

The car says, *I am the master of my destiny*; the train says, *we're
all in this together.* I might sometimes doubt the second, but
the daily carnage testifies to the absolute untruth of the first.

§

Looking back through the notebooks . . . in certain paragraphs,
I seem so much older than I am now; yet two years later
the same hand is executing nothing but idiocies. We must
hope that something advances in what we forlornly call the
meantime, and that the soul has its own universities.

§

Whatever they write, the conversations of the wise revolve
around exceptions, and the more one knows and connects,
the less seems exceptional; hence the taciturnity that is the
hallmark of all halfway decent thinkers.

Sometimes I wonder if there is an invisible amanuensis on hand at the beginning of our love affairs, scribbling down the improvisations of the first few hours. Too often it seems that they provide the entire script of the melodrama to come, from which we soon find ourselves incapable of straying a word.

§

I finish an enormous book of prayers drawn from every major world religion (I refuse to believe there are any more of the damn things); good to have a prejudice confirmed: prayer really is the lowest form of literature. Desire and flattery are nowhere sung so nakedly.

§

We were meant to make a child and did not allow ourselves to, over and over again. In the end our lovemaking could not shake the taint of *mortification*; of all the things, of all the things.

§

Mercifully, there is always one writer who seems to scupper our chances of originality. The truly original are unreadable: Joyce became so as soon as his debt was paid to Ibsen.

§

At the extremes of sexual behaviour, the difference in the projects is still apparent: men are frequently trying to bludgeon themselves into insensibility, women trying to bludgeon themselves into feeling something.

The reader may be witness to the exchange, but can never participate in it; poetry, in the end, is a private transaction between the author and the Void. The poem is firstly a spiritual courtesy, the act of returning a borrowed book.

§

Whether we die idiots or sages will depend on the direction of the wind. Wisdom is not an accumulated virtue, but rather an unpredictable weather through which the mind passes. We wouldn't long survive if the cloud cover of our ignorance were permanently dispelled, and the sun allowed to blaze through our days: we don't have the skin for it.

§

Art can almost be defined as the practice of solving scientific problems without recourse to scientific method. The distance between the stars is traversed only by the artistic imagination; the bird of paradise flutters into life in the hands of a bored sailor. The trisection of the angle, employing only a straight edge and a pair of compasses, is, according to Wantzel's irrefutable proof, perfectly impossible. The solution, of course, is to discard the instruments and execute it freehand.

It's only in falling short of the Great Work that we attain anything worthwhile at all. Equip yourself for the summit, and you might stand a half-decent chance of reaching the foothills ... How many frozen and starved corpses do we stumble over in the outlying forests, men and women who have perished for want of the equipment even a modest ambition would have supplied them?

§

Sympathetic proof of hylozoism: imagine a stone lying on a beach, undisturbed for fifty years; impossible to think that, walking by, we could pick it up and throw it into the sea, and that it could feel *nothing* ...

§

W., the long perfect whiteness of her, into which we were all intruders.

§

I can never think of the time I spend idling in railway stations as lost; it's a waiting liberated from the three temporal vices of regret, anticipation and boredom, the weak echo of that bliss spent between lifetimes.

I always find myself drawing a thick black line down the gutter of the notebook. I suppose the presence of the abyss, however vestigial, prepares an excuse for all the absent felicities, as well as those monsters which occasionally claw their way up to the page . . .

§

The most erotic things that can be done to you are those that are driven by the purest selfishness on the part of your lover. Charity, on the other hand, is the great anaphrodisiac.

§

I would lie for hours, foetal and agonised with boredom, because – I now learn from my mother – they had taken my books away, having realised being sent to my room was no punishment at all. In the next twenty years I spent more time accumulating books than reading them. Now two lifetimes couldn't read them, or four trucks take them away, or a hundred mothers. Though that one revelation was enough to frighten me off seeking the roots of my other manias.

§

No comfort to the roll call of my deceived, but my duplicities have destroyed me, that is to say, succeeded. Even the singularity of *me* now seems an impossible presumption. I couldn't lose myself to the light, so I lost myself to the lie. One of our several great Western . . . alternatives.

The insane enthusiasm of a nursery gardener who prunes his roses long before they flower, even the very buds . . . The brutal aesthetic of the bare branch and the thorn . . . To think what a vicious, perfect bloom this strain would immediately bring forth were we to simply *allow* it!

§

Exclams are for hysterics! Ellipses are for sensitives . . . Colons are for bullies. Please: can we either have *all* the punctuation, or none? We are about forty characters short. I want *degrees* of italics.

§

The tannery is the best place to conceal a fart; the university, an ignorance . . . A man should bury the worst of his private sins in common atrocities, like the proverbial wise murderer, dragging the corpse of his victim onto the moonlit battlefield.

§

It's a singularly bizarre phenomenon that after the first encounter, the face of the beloved-to-be cannot be retrieved. In our mind's eye, we hold the dinner table of the previous evening, and though we can sweep from guest to guest, fixing in turn the thin-lipped novelist, the drunken critic, the wall-eyed accountant and his horse-faced wife – however desperately we try to call back her features, there she sits, her face as perfectly bright and blank as if she had spent the entire evening with a mirror held up in its place.

Any idea born out of nothing but the leisure in which to think it will ultimately, whatever its ingenuity and elegance, be revealed as perfectly superfluous.

§

If I do not constantly evince an attitude of self-disgust, it's due to nothing more than a lack of stamina.

§

If we expect our work to survive our death even by a single day, we should stop defending it this minute, that it might sooner learn its self-sufficiency.

§

Every year they all accept the honours, the Marxists, the punks, the republicans . . . The excuses, at least, have to show some imagination. (The poets tend to mumble, pleadingly, 'It honours the form.' As if the form needed it, and from this. Far nobler to say, 'I did it for my mother.') To all of which one replies, 'No: it has neutralised such tiny threat as you once presented.' Vanity, our one chrome-plated corruption.

§

In hell even the trees are not blameless. *Particularly* the trees.

My blind fury at J.'s obituaries, as he denied me the profound pleasure of being jealous of him any longer . . . though even in death, I could still discern the cast of ambition in his face. No doubt he's already making his way up the infernal ladder, and has risen to some subaltern of the demonic.

§

In that short walk to the bathroom at three in the morning, I realised that, caught at the right hour, I would have little trouble giving up the flesh. I regarded myself as a perfect stranger; I was no more than a ghost with a full bladder.

§

Our names should be lengthened a little after our demise, by the lovely matronymic of death . . . we'd then appear in the conversation of our friends and enemies with our signature cadence gently altered, discreetly informing strangers of our change of status.

§

Every motive, being a different admixture of *every* desire a man or woman possesses, is almost infinitely complex. The failing of all legislators: their inability to see that no one ever acts for one reason alone.

Every morning the writer should go to the window, look out and remind himself that aside from his own species, not one thing he sees – not one bird, tree or stone – has in its possession the name he gives it.

§

Hell is an enforced solitude, heaven a voluntary one.

§

Once, on a long train journey, she taught me to *sign*. It was itself a cruel mime of a request, one she knew to be nearly impossible for me: to pursue her with silence.

§

The worst atrocities are committed by the absolutists, who don't understand that dishonourable circumstances challenge you to behave with more honour than ever. It is no insanity for them to flip cheerfully between the obligations of the family hearth and the death camp. The most human project is *mitigation*.

§

Our most grievous error is to think our incarnation some kind of cosmic privilege. We fall into time as a dead leaf into a river.

Reality is just the name that we give to everything that happens to face up.

§

In art, the only true crime of ignorance is the rediscovery of the cliché. The flower of genius, on the other hand, is the *innovation* of the cliché – being the revelation of what we hadn't known we'd *always* known.

§

I knew in those moments who owned the eyes, but not the stare. The stare belonged to no one, and had instead arrived as a kind of paraclete, a radiant ghost, falling among us as He had promised, as two gathered together in the Name.

§

To leave the page covered, and the silence intact; to *enforce* that silence in the reader's life for the duration of the poem . . .

§

An unnamed literary plagiarist is described in the press as a 'confidence trickster'. Aye, that *really* narrows it down.

Sentimental art tries to provoke emotions of which we should already be in high possession. What kind of poetry *should* be made for those who require more than flat testimony to be moved by an Auschwitz?

§

Don't delude yourself that this watery, carbon-based arrangement will persist any longer than necessary. Having failed to locate the soul in the heart, liver, or pineal gland, in a hidden corner of the hypothalamus, or in some probability field in quantum space – we nonetheless still host it, or the dream of it, and it will set up house just as happily in the motherboards of our scions.

§

My obsession with computers (what an infancy they're in, and how it *charms*!) is a kind of nostalgia for the future. I long to be half-man, half-desk.

§

Sleeping with your own muse is an unpardonable breach of literary protocol. But to sleep with a friend's, and tell him about it, is to do him the greatest favour as an artist.

§

She was not comfortable with the idea of him alone in her house, less for those secrets of hers he might discover than for the lack of them. The lack was, in fact, her worst secret.

He had thought to brand her with his child, knowing her the one thing he could not bear to lose; she had thought to escape him with her child, knowing him the one thing that might possess her.

§

If only poets and novelists could be translated into *musicianhood*, even for a few seconds; then we'd see the vast majority, after only a few notes, revealed as a bunch of desperate scrapers and parpers without a tune in their heads, or the rudiments of technique. God, the *time* we would save . . .

§

All our instruments are accurate, except the clock. The clock holds up two sticks in the air and draws a conclusion.

§

A life lived in the margins and footnotes of what he might have been . . . His epitaph: *He digressed.*

Most people are convinced that the path of the departing spirit is distinguished by its scatter of holy detritus (they are forever producing bits of shiny rubbish as evidence of His recent passing); but the one thing of which God is incapable is fragmentation. The path He has taken is distinguished only by its godlessness. When we stumble upon anything – a bottle of wine, a poem, a poor suburb, a railway platform – that is incontestably the worst of its kind, we know for certain that we have picked up the trail again.

§

In all beautifully expressed tautologies there is a grain of gold that is surplus. This reliable alchemy applies to all the arts that obey the chrysometric laws, that cut with the golden blade. Philosophy – which cuts with the silver, and works on isometric principles – always falls a grain short. The true poem picks up the gold thread of the hem of the robe of the departing spirit, the glittering clew in the dark woods that will lead us back into the light. The true philosophy delineates the precise nature of its own failure; therefore, knowing the exact form of *deus absconditus,* we can recognise the godless trail when we stumble across it, and start our pursuit.

§

In her, I realised I had finally given myself up to what I always professed was my true study: *the interpretation of silence.* I think perhaps I'd fancied it a fusion of psychoacoustics and critical theory. Immediately I was immersed in Hermes Trismegistus and Aleister Crowley.

I have no more ambition for this book than that some day someone will be lying in bed and read out a single line – and that their companion will turn away from them in silence . . .

§

The sea rehearses all possible landscapes, the sky all possible seas. But the land is a lexicon of frozen hells, and some of us remember.

§

The language of the angels and of the blessed consists of a single verb, possessing an infinite number of tenses, moods and conjugations. In the language of the damned, every word is a part of speech entirely unrelated to any other; this tongue is the subject of enforced study for those wretches who, under the scourge of the infernal grammarians, are condemned forever to the memorisation of vast and endless textbooks. The two languages are, of course, precisely the same, the only difference being that this knowledge is withheld from the latter party.

§

The *emphasis* is all wrong; the tale of his life will read like a great book underlined by an idiot.

Critical theory – a whole subject devised for no other purpose than the stimulation of underemployed or unemployable intellects – is incapable of accepting a straightforwardly *boring* solution to anything, regardless of how correct it might prove. It would contradict its status as a *pastime*.

§

Most etymologies lie forever buried from sight. Words are locked tombs in which the corpses still lie breathing.

§

Rusted to the shape of their ideology, the brains of most political demagogues are like a stopped clock; the most dangerous limit their public appearances to twice a day, knowing that they'd be revealed as lunatics at any other hour.

§

Poetry is the word in silence. Only a poem can consist of one word.

§

The gods know that fane-building is the first step towards their banishment; so they are always absent from their temples. What we love about churches, what continues to draw us into them, is their perfect emptiness.

There is one thing, at least, which everyone regards as the dullest point of common knowledge, the details of which – by tact, providence, but most likely chance – have been withheld from you. So you will discover, too late in the day, why your house was sold to you so cheaply, or the *real* ingredients of the communion host, or that all left-handed males are culled in their fiftieth year . . .

§

I love the way we all suddenly stop traducing our enemy when we hear they have a cancer or have suffered a stroke. If only we could always keep in the front of our minds that we are *all* dying.

§

The true avant-garde cultivate the territories others merely staked out, and are the real subversives among us, since they never draw attention to themselves through the crime of originality.

§

The poet's only consolation is the thought that somewhere, right now, there is a man or woman of far greater intelligence making a complete buffoon of themselves as they labour over the composition of a simple couplet.

A vital component of the awe we feel before a work of art is the knowledge that we could never make it ourselves. In this way the artist, through his or her superhuman technique, is permitted to impersonate God or His sublimities – and through this deception the audience is brought more closely into His real presence. But the more democratised the practice becomes, the further this reflected presence retreats, until we're left in moonless night. The end result of the Modernist project: the proscenium arch evaporates, the stage sinks to the floor, the curtains unravel and we're brought face to face with nothing but our own mediocrity. What else can we do but embrace it as a brother? Our affectionate recognition, however, conceals our utter lack of *amazement*.

§

Taking a lover often solves the sexual difficulties of a marriage, if only because it becomes pointless to imagine yourself *elsewhere*.

§

In the true artist there is no more progression than in the true art.

§

There are men and women who talk so seamlessly of themselves you wonder when they managed to listen long enough to have acquired the power of speech in the first place.

We grow into our prophecies. Often it is the simple embarrassment of having told everyone we will leave our lover that gives us the courage to do so; but this example calls a deeper system from the shadows. Usually we must open up the path before we can follow it, the air standing – all too often – solid against us. On those occasions we send out the god in ourselves, and follow his empty trail to our salvation. This is why transition so often feels like abandonment.

§

'She sought balance in everything', though to a pathological degree. A lull in the conversation would turn her into a kind of witty hysteric; but the most long-winded bore would also find her his perfect listener. In occupations that should have required no thought, she would tackle the databases and spreadsheets with the energy and imagination of a Turing or Frege, but crashed out of two of the best universities a few weeks after matriculation. If pursued, she would disappear from the face of the earth; but she proposed to him three times, so perfect was his play of requiring nothing of her.

§

So perfect was his play of requiring nothing of her, she proposed to him three times. Naturally, he refused; or rather, said nothing. Only when she was lost to him did he break down and articulate – or at least *sign* – his need. For some, only the losses can be acknowledged; they draw up their accounts, both their credits and debits, only in negative integers.

Art is the prism by which the white light – that synaesthetic radiance that we usually indicate with the word *truth* – is diffracted into its constituent frequencies. But the process isn't perfect, and in true art there is always a little chromatic bleed: we hear a little music in every painting, a little poetry in every song. False art, having no illumination in the first place, is notable for precisely this lack of *suggestiveness*.

§

The first procedure of good style is the inversion of the form in which the idea occurred to the thinker.

§

Most relationships that begin in deceit end the same way. Our inamorata will never forget the duplicity of which she knows us to be capable. That knowledge soon becomes an expectation, the expectation becomes a prophesy; and in the end, most prophesies compel their own fulfilment. No better example of the way in which karma operates *within* our lives, as well as across the interstices.

§

Music has the most exact *science* of all the arts. When we hear a note in our heads and attempt to replicate it with our voice or on the piano, our nearest miss is the most disastrous choice we could have made; someone else will come along and hit a note a whole fifth out, with far less discordant consequences. In no other art is this the case – the use of the near-synonym, or the slightly inappropriate pigment, jars only with those deeply attuned to the medium, who perhaps already perceive it as a form of music, a form of pure vibration.

[189]

Dinner, and the usual dreadful updates: L.'s cancer, P.'s accident, M.'s stillbirth . . . Yet the only thing that draws a real gasp from me is the news that R.'s library has burned down.

§

The most flattering compliments are paid by people who clearly don't know us well enough; nonetheless, we invariably make the mistake of acquainting ourselves with the flatterer that we might hear more. Inevitably, upon that closer acquaintance, the flattery evaporates, and even the original compliment is withdrawn.

§

God's demise: a suicide, surely, if all those reports of it had observed the first poetic imperative, the consistency of the conceit. In which case (before we enter in to more delightful speculation, such as what new limbo he had to prepare for himself in advance) what exactly was his *method?* Though having tried and failed with his starry ligatures and inhaled nebulae, it was no doubt the one thing of which he found himself incapable. The best he could manage was to *fake it* – and being in possession of the one thing he could envy, we were the first to be duped. We are, in fact, his suicide note.

§

To the man who has heard nothing but Bach, everything else he subsequently hears puts him a little in mind of Bach. Bad critics often conceive of similarities that owe nothing to the works themselves and everything to the paucity of examples they have to draw on; their ignorance insists on them.

The world disappointed me as soon as I got here. I'm proud of having *lost no time*.

§

We could easily have evolved eyelids thick enough to block out the light; but we're not yet *safe*.

§

One thing all adulterers will tell you: the dreaded return to the marital bed turns out to be such a simple and easy deception, it stands as a far more grave indictment of the spirit than the original misdemeanour ever was.

§

The successful impersonation of intelligence often leads to more original thought than the casual operation of the real thing, as it better comprehends the artifice of the idea – and is therefore not constrained by any attempt, unconscious or otherwise, at naturalism.

§

I considered myself immune to the sirens of suicide, until one morning I somehow managed to alert myself to a grievous sea change; the idea had just crossed my mind *casually*. Since that moment I have been roped to the mast of myself.

I occasionally have these anachronistic fantasies where I acquaint Bach with the midi sequencer, Borges with the internet, da Vinci with digital imaging . . . though such things might have dismantled them, as realisations of their necessary *impossibles.*

§

Death will shock us only in its familiarity.

§

As soon as we attempt to recreate the brilliancies of the previous evening, we are lost. We invariably forget how they depended upon the dullness of the conversation or the odd receptivity of our interlocutor. We should leave all gems where we find them, their lustre being drawn only from their nondescript matrix and the peculiarity of the light at the time.

§

The secret of labour is to find the vocation in which we are as lost and as driven as in our lovemaking. No one ever thinks of the calories they expend there as *work.*

§

Nothing could rescue me from the infinite doubt of the instant, no reassurance, no recollection of any previous instant, however recent. She had reduced me to a form of infantilism; the abyss of the endless present. One hour's radio silence, and she was the Silent Mother and I was in hell.

I knew, in the end, that I could addict her to nothing, to no vanity, to no compliment, to no pain – and that this had always been my only strategy. In all matters of love I had never amounted to more than a *pusher*.

§

Anything that elicits an immediate nod of recognition has only reconfirmed a prejudice.

§

I first kissed her in a doorway in Victoria; I last kissed her in a doorway in Victoria. No city allows us to haunt ourselves like London, to contrive such insane symmetries, to find ourselves yet again – years later, seemingly *against all odds* – at the same tiny coordinate in its vast districts. We turn the corner, and the light will suddenly break in on a dark hall, filled with our crossed swords, our mouldering trophies, our ragged tapestries.

§

Just as men can fuck better on a full bladder, it's better to write with some part of the mind preoccupied with matters other than those immediately at hand; in matters where there is no *real* urgency, it's often worthwhile importing one arbitrarily. I'm most likely to deliver the line I have waited for all morning five minutes before I have to run for a train.

Desire is the inconvenience of its object. Lourdes isn't Lourdes if you live in Lourdes.

§

No matter how intolerable an event was, it only has to be repeated three times for you to invest it with a little nostalgia.

§

There can be no such thing, in our human experience, as seamless progress. The descent from Beachy Head will have its lighter moments; even the road to hell will have stretches more bearable – which we will succeed in construing as more *pleasant* – than others. We're cursed by these, since they continually give rise to hope.

§

Silence is our only bravery. If 'literary courage' isn't an oxymoron – perhaps it only consists in realising that you've had your last word on the subject and leaving it at that.

As a compositional practice, music is easily superior to poetry in that it can be exercised at will. The composer is often detained in nothing more than the business of making a single large and subtle calculation – the emotion consequently registered in the heart of the listener having at no point in the process necessarily been felt in his own. This is unthinkable in poetry, yet more often than not – whatever the agonies or raptures of the poet – the reader is left dry-eyed and perfectly indifferent. But to have felt *nothing*, and *still devastate an audience*; that sensation is probably as close to divinity as we will get.

§

Man is only a biological interlude in a much longer narrative, but *knowing* the fact of his intermediacy between the mineral and the bodiless seraphim makes his condition a sentence, a term. No wonder we count the days the way we do, like no other beast.

§

Cioran talks of the shame of not being a musician. It's a less resonant omission, but he should have been grateful he never bore the disgrace of being merely an *average* one.

§

A poem is a little machine for remembering itself.

Since it was never their birthright, the working classes are rarely in unselfconscious possession of their intelligence; they regard it precisely as they do their bank account, obsessed with its fluctuations, its variable reserves, and wait with trepidation for every cheque written against it to clear. Even when their account is in rude health, the *pride* they take in it is an obscenity – flashing the gold cards of their Joyce, their Epictetus and their Derrida at the least opportunity, to cover the cost of conversational trifles.

§

If we know we will forgive at some point in the future, we should forgive now; if we intend to stop hating, stop now. Which is really to say that since we will die, we should die now, and act at least in part as ghosts, with their equanimity and detachment.

AFTERWORD: ON APHORISMS

NOTES ON SOME APHORISTS

CANETTI

He did not really understand the aphoristic form. In an intelligence like his, this should tell us something of the obscurity of the skill. ('Rarity' might imply it had a value.)

CHESTERTON

The only really great aphorist in English. Halifax is okay, but all the rest – Hazlitt and (curiously) Wilde excepted – are *wits*. The anglophone embarrassment over the unsubstantiated assertion – which the English, especially, cannot help thinking of as a subset of 'wisdom literature' – began very early. This it sees as the sole preserve of the holy books; all other attempts at it are laughed away uncomfortably, on the grounds of their seedy human provenance. You would think such a culturally ingrained self-hatred would make the British ideal aphorists. However you can be overqualified for the task.

CIORAN

The Buddha, let's remember, *required* our scepticism; Cioran, possibly alone among European writers, refined it to attain a kind of terrible, insomniac enlightenment. Like Borges, he managed to turn a European tongue against itself to approach ideas that (unlike Pali, say) it had no right to – and somehow contrive their ghostly appearance, like the animated figures in a zootrope; the result is something like Nagarjuna's Western reincarnation. To read him as a Westerner is thus to be a little reprogrammed. No wonder that he is considered, in this age of the pseudoscience, no philosopher, and absent from almost all contemporary accounts of the subject. He wrote only in obsolete genres. But by comparison, everything else seems to be already stalked by its own critical refutation – backed into punctilious consistency, supporting references, and an irrefutable (i.e. wholly circular) systematism before it has even begun to articulate its position.

COCTEAU

He would have been the greatest, but he was far too happy.
The dominant harmony and black dissonance supplied by
heterosexual self-loathing are the only things I really miss in
Barthes, too.

HERACLITUS

To read him for the first time is like digging a hundred knives
from the ground, all of them still gleaming.

JABÈS

A great *writer*, but as an aphorist a peculiar cocktail
of rabbinical proverbialism, French blur and poetic
overstatement. Contrary to popular belief, there is nothing *self-
evident* about aphoristic truth. Within the form, the axiom and
the crazy assertion are the same waste of breath.

KRAUS

Too much spleen over sense, and Marx's fatal attraction for
rhetorical chiasmus, which is always fake; only forms can
be placed in such symmetries, never concepts. And for a
genuine lover of women to have affected Schopenhauer's and
Nietzsche's *misogyny*, of all their attributes . . . *You guys.*

LA BRUYÈRE

A lexicon of human prejudice. Still useful.

LA ROCHEFOUCAULD

In an old Penguin Classic edition of his work, a superbly bad-
tempered back-cover blurb used him to demolish a stupid
contemporary critic. Any writer who can be set so easily to his
own defence must earn our respect.

LEOPARDI

I wish we could suppress this Romantic habit of ours of
automatically conferring genius upon even the tardiest of early
deaths.

LICHTENBERG
German *concision?* He deserves even more credit than we give him.

NIETSZCHE
All his famous contradictions disappear as soon as you remember to read him as *literature*, which isn't obliged to be coherent.

PASCAL
More and more he reads like Confucius, i.e. an axiomatic redundancy. This probably pays him the highest compliment; every discipline needs its Euclid.

PESSOA
Oh, but everyone loves the *idea* of Pessoa.

PORCHIA
Possibly the greatest, as almost no one has read him. But if his words are all that survives of us, we will have done well.

RIGAUT
I read of Jacques Rigaut that 'he demoralised whatever came into contact with him'. I have done my bit, to be sure, though generally only with other humans. But, through mere *propinquity*, to plunge a dog into despair, a *nightstand* . . . I am quivering with professional jealousy.

ST THOMAS GOSPEL
The Nazarene Cynic laid bare, but somehow St Thomas still comes out of it better.

SIMMEL
Perhaps he *is* one of the greats. His work is far too boring for us ever to be able to tell.

STEVENS

Amateurism is generally a huge advantage to a poet, but this led him only to write the first half of his aphorisms. He omits the *proof.* For the genuine amateur, the slightest literary obligation smacks of a journalistic deadline.

TALEB

As an aphorist he is *nearly* good, which is pretty good these days. But his voice always quivers on the last word, like the bully and sentimentalist he knows he is.

VALÉRY

If he has one fault, it is that you could always tell he composed his aphorisms horizontally. They taste a little too milky at times, a little too much of sleep.

WEIL

Weil's and Arendt's almost inadvertent dalliances apart, women have so far found very little use for the aphorism, far and away the most troubling indictment we can serve against *any* form.

WEININGER

A warning to the young. He is rendered largely worthless through his youthful desperation to have reality fit modish typologies. For the intellectuals of the *fin-de-siècle* to the 1930s, anti-semitism was primarily a way to simplify matters. But we must remember he was only a child, and the son of a Jewish goldsmith.

A poem is a ladder to the sky; an aphorism just a stair to the cellar. But right now there is probably more you need in the cellar than in the sky.

§

On the morning the Barbarians wandered through the gates, everyone in Rome had their feet up and was reading a book of aphorisms.

§

Five rules: an aphorism must

1) be short, but not fragmentary;
2) be free-standing, but not extraneous;
3) speak from no authority but its own;
4) be original, but not novel;
5) be self-verifying, but not self-evident.

Five stylistic errors:

1) Authority is not arrogated to oneself merely through the bold use of the copula.
2) Remember – whoever you *think* you're imitating, those italics are Nietzsche's, and he was a lunatic.
3) No one wants your damn advice.
4) An aphorism can be paraphrased, but never abridged; poems, vice versa. (Poets will tell you their poem can't be abridged either, but rarely feel that way about anyone else's.)
5) A bad poem appears to betray the author's smallness of spirit; a bad aphorism, their want of wit. The truth is that they reveal absolutely nothing beyond a lack of talent for the form, but by then it's all too late.

§

Even in its bleakest shades, the poem has a redemptive air. The aphorism is relieved of that cultural burden, and allows the reader to relax into the knowledge that nothing will save them.

§

The aphorists' symposium ended in broad agreement, which is to say in complete disaster.

§

Leafing through something called *3000 Inspirational Quotes* at least helped clarify my aim. I dream of a book of irresistible calls to inaction.

Suddenly I realised I had written three books of aphorism where none should have sufficed.

§

My fellow scholars, certainly; my fellow poets . . . possibly. But *aphorists*? Why the hell would I want to share the last word?

§

Writing aphorisms feels like doing vital work in complete secrecy, a fantasy one can best indulge when doing irrelevant work in total obscurity.

§

Like poetry, aphorism is also mode of reading. We decide in advance to discover a general truth. Thus, found on a box of matches: *keep away from damp places and small children.*

§

The aphorism is an end in itself.

§

The aphorism is an *idea* for an aphorism.

Both poets and philosophers have traditions which equate truth and brevity, and they meet again at the aphorism, that pre-Socratic intersection where they can stand around offering mutual commiserations on their cultural irrelevance.

§

If one or two of these have been accidentally repeated, I hope it will be taken as a sign of their being utterly unmemorable, even for their author. Though the reader will also find this an advantage when I occasionally say something they would rather forget.

§

They asked me to write a weekly aphorism column for the newspaper, so I submitted a few. They were returned as too obscure. Could I do something topical? I wrote a couple on the week's events. Could I do something funnier? I replied with what I thought was a witty one-liner. 'But it's just a joke!' they cried. At which point I realised they didn't know what an aphorism *was*: they had merely hoped it was something else.

§

You say *ay*-phorism, I say *ah*-phorism; let's call the whole thing pointless.

§

Copula shmopula.

Each poem has its inspiration, each aphorism its offence.

§

A poem assuages. The aphorism merely scratches. But you don't assuage an itch.

§

Poet: someone in the aphorism game for the money.

§

The aphorism always gives me the delightful sensation of fiddling with my opus posthumous.

§

The aphorism: hindsight with murderous purpose. *Esprit de l'escalier,* but on the *ascent.*

§

Of *course* all these amount to nothing. Their collation might be my error; their aggregation, however, is yours.

§

The aphorism will often contain one italicised word; this denotes its magnetic North, not the direction it's heading.

Key: read *I* for *he*; *R.* for *S.; no one* for *you; it* for I.

§

The shorter the form, the greater our expectation of its significance – and the greater its capacity for disappointing us. A book of aphorisms is a lexicon of disappointments. The form's only virtue is its brevity; at least the reader cannot seriously hold that it has wasted their time.

§

The relief I found in reading a terrible aphorist! I had begun to wonder if brevity was in itself some sort of unassailable virtue.

§

The aphorism is a *brief* waste of time. The poem is a *complete* waste of time. The novel is a *monumental* waste of time.

§

The aphorism is nobody speaking to nobody; it's less read than eavesdropped upon. God knows, it's barely even *written:* I disown them immediately.

§

Despite our attempts to imbue them with some flavour, *any* flavour – aphorisms all turn out so . . . generic; they all sound as if they were delivered by the same disenfranchised, bad-tempered minor deity.

For years I had resisted starting work on a new book of aphorisms. I was waiting for signs of *advance*. When I finally realised nothing could be less appropriate to the form, I could begin again.

§

The aphorism is the rational articulation of a fleeting hysteria.

§

S. has written a *comprehensive* book of aphorisms. He has made a vast list of subjects, then sat down and composed his brilliancy on each of them – even those on which he had no opinion, until that very moment.

§

How many aphorists *does* it take to change a light bulb? How many aphorists does it take to *change* a light bulb? . . . And so on with our little antipoetry, our ear to the strongbox of the line while we work the combinations, trying the italics on one word, then the next, until we hear something weaken inside . . .

§

A book of aphorisms makes no pretence to engage the reader in any sort of dialogue; to judge by its tone of relentless asseveration, it *has no opinion of them*. What the reader feels is a kind of *ultimate* contempt: that of ink for the human, the mineral for the animal.

X has numbered his aphorisms. Now he has added a *cumulative* disappointment.

§

Poetic truth occurs at that point in the steady refinement of a form of words where they cease to be paraphrasable, but have not yet become purely oracular. Also, perhaps, a definition of the aphorism, its talentless, tone-deaf brother.

§

An aphorism might be prompted by a wise or idiotic action, but it can rarely provide the weather to engender or avert others. Aphorisms are as useful as precis of poems, as entertaining as descriptions of jokes. Their conclusions are too general. Only specificities breed others.

§

I no longer mean all of these. I meant them once. Some of them *only* once.

§

The difference between the aphorism and the poem is that the aphorism states its conclusion first. It is a form without tension, and therefore simultaneously perfect and perfectly dispensable. There is no road, no tale, no desire.

Reading a book of aphorisms diligently in the sequence they appear makes about as much sense as eating a large jar of onions diligently in the sequence they appear; and no one should try to finish either in one sitting.

§

Of course you don't like all the aphorisms. I don't like all of *you*.

§

Why so many aphorisms on aphorisms? Only an ant can correct the manners of an ant.

§

Whatever else, each aphorism also speaks death to the system. That is to say *my creed*, could such a thing exist.

§

There is a makeweight of lies or conjecture in any statement longer than a sentence, longer than a breath, longer than that which can inhabit the present moment.

§

To induce a horrific paralysis of boredom in the reader, in the compass of *one sentence* . . .

I would make her the Clodia, the Laura, the goddamn *Beatrice* of the aphorism. Now *there* was a gratitude I would have to explain to her.

§

Fragments, indeed. As if there were anything to break.

§

The aphorism is already a shadow of itself.